# EAT
# YOURSELF
# HAPPY

# EAT YOURSELF
# HAPPY

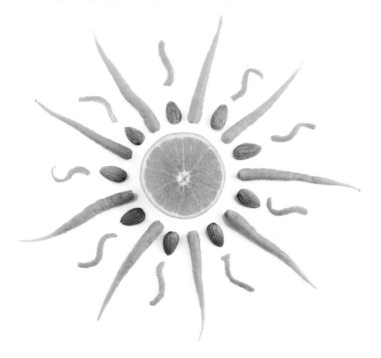

## INGREDIENTS & RECIPES
## FOR A GOOD MOOD, EVERY DAY

### GILL PAUL
**NUTRITIONIST: KAREN SULLIVAN, ASET, VTCT, BSC**

hamlyn

An Hachette UK Company
www.hachette.co.uk

First published in Great Britain in 2014 by Hamlyn,
a division of Octopus Publishing Group Ltd
Endeavour House
189 Shaftesbury Avenue
London WC2H 8JY
www.octopusbooks.co.uk

Distributed in U.S. by Hachette Book Group USA,
237 Park Avenue, New York NY 10017 USA
www.octopusbooksusa.com

Distributed in Canada by Canadian Manda Group,
165 Dufferin Street, Toronto, Ontario,
Canada M6K 3HG

ISBN 978-0-60062-705-0

A CIP catalog record for this book is available from
the Library of Congress

Printed and bound in China

10 9 8 7 6 5 4 3 2 1

All reasonable care has been taken in the
preparation of this book but the information
it contains is not intended to take the place of
treatment by a qualified medical practitioner.

People with known nut allergies should avoid
recipes containing nuts or nut derivatives,
and vulnerable people should avoid dishes
containing raw or lightly cooked eggs.

Standard level kitchen spoon and cup
measurements are used in all recipes.

Ovens should be preheated to the specified
temperature—if using a convection oven,
follow the manufacturer's instructions for
adjusting the time and temperature. Medium eggs
should be used unless otherwise stated.

Some of the recipes in this book have previously
appeared in other titles published by Hamlyn.

**Editor:** Jo Wilson
**Copy-editing:** Jo Smith
**Art Director:** Jonathan Christie
**Photographic Art Direction, Prop Styling
and Design:** Isabel de Cordova
**Photography:** Will Heap
**Food Styling:** Joy Skipper
**Picture Library Manager:** Jen Veall
**Assistant Production Manager:** Caroline Alberti

# CONTENTS

# INTRODUCTION

We all feel down from time to time. It's the natural response to sad news, such as a layoff, relationship breakdown, or serious illness affecting us or someone we love. However, some people are more prone to depression than others; they get down more often and then have trouble getting their mood back onto an even keel. For a minority, the depression is so severe they require medical help, such as medication or therapy, just to get through the week.

When we are down, we tend to opt for the wrong kinds of foods, choosing sugary foods for a quick burst of energy and alcoholic drinks to dull the pain, yet these things make depression worse. There are dozens of different types of depression, with different causes, but almost all are improved by eating the right kinds of foods to synthesize ample supplies of brain neurotransmitters, address vitamin and mineral deficiencies, and stabilize blood sugar levels. No matter how low you feel, wise food choices will make you feel happier, and the benefits will start immediately.

### What makes us feel low?

There are a number of factors that affect mood. Genetics play a part; you are more likely to experience depression if one of your parents had depression. Difficult childhood experiences, such as sexual abuse, bullying, or the loss of a parent or sibling, can also make you more prone to depression when you are older. And certain personality types get depressed more often than others—for example, those with low self-esteem. Scientists are also aware that our biochemistry plays a major role in affecting our moods. MRI (magnetic resonance imaging) scans made of the brains of people who have depression indicate that there may be deficiencies of certain neurotransmitters (the chemicals responsible for passing on signals). Hormonal imbalances can also trigger depression, which is why some women get depressed and anxious when their estrogen levels drop before periods or during menopause. Lack of sunlight is an additional factor that can make us depressed, because sunshine stimulates estrogen, serotonin, and the synthesis of vitamin D.

# How to eat yourself happy

### 1. Eat enough protein

Some key amino acids, the building blocks of proteins, must be included in our diets because we can't manufacture them ourselves. For example, the amino acid tryptophan is required to make serotonin, the neurotransmitter that controls mood, sleep patterns, and appetite. Likewise phenylalanine is essential for the production of noradrenaline and adrenaline, which affect energy levels, and dopamine, which regulates the emotions. Eating a wide range of good-quality proteins, and including protein in at least two meals or snacks a day, will help to make sure that you produce enough of these all important, mood-balancing neurotransmitters.

### 2. Top up the B vitamins

Those with low levels of B vitamins (especially $B_6$, $B_{12}$, and folate) are at greater risk of depression, because these substances are required to keep the nervous system healthy and control the production and balance of neurotransmitters. Eating plenty of bananas, avocados, chicken, whole-grain products, and leafy green vegetables will help to replenish your stores.

### 3. Feast on fish

Those who eat a lot of fish are less prone to depression than those who don't. It's because the omega-3 oils found in fish, particularly one called EPA, help to build brain cell connections and receptor sites for neurotransmitters. The more EPA in your blood, the more serotonin you will make—and the happier you'll be.

### 4. Choose the right carbs

The types of carbohydrates we eat affect our mood and behavior. Avoid refined carbohydrates, such as white bread, white pasta, white rice, and all processed foods, and cut down on your sugar intake to even out blood sugar levels, prevent dips in energy, and reduce mood swings. Don't be tempted to avoid carbs altogether, however,

because they are necessary for many crucial processes in the body, including the manufacture of serotonin. Opt for unprocessed carbs with plenty of fiber that will be absorbed more slowly into the digestive system and have less of an effect on blood sugar. That means eating plenty of whole grains, brown rice, beans, and vegetables.

## 5. Look after your digestion

It's long been known that stress and anxiety can cause problems in the digestive tract, but recent research has suggested that it also works the other way around, and digestive problems can be responsible for triggering depression. Combat this by eating foods that encourage healthy digestion, such as plenty of fiber and yogurt with live cultures to replenish bacteria in the digestive tract. You should aim to drink plenty of water every day, too.

## 6. Dose up with vitamin D

Vitamin D deficiency can also trigger depression. We get vitamin D through the food we eat and through exposure to sunlight on our skin. Optimize your chances of beating depression by eating plenty of vitamin-D-rich foods (such as oily fish and eggs) and getting out into daylight as much as you can.

## 7. Avoid caffeine and alcohol

Caffeine drinks (coffee, tea, and colas) stimulate the release of insulin, which mops up sugar in the blood, causing lowered levels of sugar and giving you an energy dip. Stick to one or two cups of coffee a day when you're feeling down. And alcohol is a depressant, so it will make it harder to come out of a depression.

## Getting started

When you are feeling low, you may experience a loss of appetite and tend to skip meals—or, conversely, you may overeat, looking for comfort in food. Looking after yourself physically is the first step to curing the blues. Make sure you eat small regular meals and snacks, which will improve symptoms rapidly by keeping your blood sugar levels stable. This should stop you from having cravings for sweet or fatty foods.

Follow the meal planner on pages 30–33 for a powerful mood booster. If you would like to address specific symptoms, such as stress, irritability, loss of libido, or sleep problems, check the problem solver on pages 26–29 for key foods you should be eating. Pages 12–25 list the foods and their benefits and give suggestions on how to incorporate them into your diet.

There are other easy ways you can make a difference. Exercise may help psychologically by boosting your self-esteem, and it is also thought to have a biochemical effect because it causes the release of endorphins, which block pain-receptor sites in the brain. Talking to other people, whether it is your doctor, a trained counselor, or a trusted friend, is also highly beneficial. The main thing is not to struggle alone. If you have been depressed most of the time for more than two weeks and it is affecting your ability to live a normal life, or if you have had any suicidal thoughts, ask your physician for help. That is what he or she is there for.

Even if your depression is not primarily caused by biochemical imbalances but is the result of genetics or life events, you should still find that eating the right foods helps. It's an all-around healthy way of eating, it's delicious—and you deserve it.

# HAPPY
# SUPERFOODS

# SUPERFOODS

These powerhouse foods help to relieve symptoms of depression and anxiety, and they will boost your health on all levels.

## Turkey

- ✔ Elevates mood
- ✔ Reduces anxiety
- ✔ Balances blood sugar levels
- ✔ Encourages a healthy nervous system
- ✔ Promotes healthy sleep

Turkey is one of the most important foods in a depression-busting diet, and its high levels of tryptophan do everything from encouraging restful sleep to boosting immunity. It is low in carbohydrates and fat but high in protein.

### It's rich in ...

- → Tryptophan, an amino acid that stimulates the production of the feel-good chemical serotonin and encourages restful sleep
- → Zinc, used to help balance blood sugar levels and boosts your immune system
- → Choline, which protects the nervous system
- → Selenium, which helps to balance moods and prevent anxiety and depression

**Use in ...** a chef's salad, with Swiss cheese, mixed greens, hard-boiled eggs, and cherry tomatoes; instead of meat balls in a tomato sauce; as a sandwich filler, mixed with lemon mayonnaise and crunchy cucumber; in a stir-fry, with Asian greens and soy sauce.

SEE: TURKEY & PEANUT NOODLE SALAD, P. 78;
CAULIFLOWER & TURKEY BIRIYANI, P. 96;
TURKEY, LENTIL & APRICOT STEW, P. 97;
THAI TURKEY BURGERS WITH CRISPY KALE, P. 98

# Sunflower seeds

✔ Elevate mood
✔ Encourage nerve health
✔ Promote healthy sleep patterns
✔ Protect against damaging effects of stress
✔ Reduce anxiety

Sunflower seeds have long been considered a natural antidepressant, and the multitude of vitamins, minerals, and other nutrients they contain make them a nutritious addition to a healthy diet and a great booster of energy and mood.

## They are rich in ...

→ Magnesium, used to regulate nerve function and balance calcium levels, encouraging restful sleep
→ Tryptophan, which enhances the production of feel-good serotonin, thus lifting mood
→ Vitamin $B_6$, used to encourage the release of the body's natural depression-fighting chemicals
→ Manganese, a component in nerve health and required for thyroid hormone production, low levels of which can lower mood

**Use in ...** trail mixes, with other seeds, nuts, and dried fruit for snacks; cereals and granola; salads and dips for extra flavor and crunch; crumble toppings; cookies and muffins, for an extra boost of healthy fats; as a coating on fish, such as sea bass.

SEE: MUESLI WITH PEACHES & YOGURT, P. 38; APPLE & CRANBERRY GRANOLA, P. 42; BANANA SUNFLOWER SEED COOKIES, P. 62; CREAMY ROASTED PEPPERS WITH MIXED GRAINS, P. 105

# Mackerel

✔ Improves mood
✔ Eases symptoms of depression
✔ Enhances energy levels
✔ Encourages relaxation
✔ Helps to treat symptoms of seasonal affective disorder (SAD)

A number of studies have found that mackerel has a significant antidepressant effect, working to boost energy levels while restoring feelings of calm and balance. Rich in healthy fats, it also plays a number of other roles in the body, encouraging good health on all levels.

## It's rich in ...

→ Omega-3 oils, which have been shown in several studies to relieve many symptoms of depression, including low mood, as well as to help regulate brain function
→ Vitamin D, used to boost immunity and make sure calcium is balanced for healthy nerve function and natural mood lift, particularly in the darker winter months
→ Magnesium, aiding nerve function and promoting relaxation and healthy sleep
→ Vitamins $B_3$ and $B_{12}$, which affect mood and other brain functions

**Use in ...** Asian salads; herbed mackerel pâtés for healthy snacks and light meals; fish cakes with lemon and herbs; cook with a harissa glaze for a North African-style dish; barbecue with ginger and lime.

SEE: MACKEREL PÂTÉ ON RYE CRISPS, P. 52; MACKEREL & ASPARAGUS TART, P. 86; MACKEREL FILLETS WITH OAT TOPPING, P. 90

## Avocado

✔ Encourages healthy brain function
✔ Helps to balance hormones
✔ Improves energy
✔ Boosts immunity
✔ Balances blood sugar
✔ Improves concentration

An excellent source of healthy fats, avocado is full of mood-boosting nutrients that can work to lift your mood while making sure of optimum health on all levels. The balance of fats, protein, and fiber helps to stabilize blood sugar levels, improving energy, stamina, and concentration.

**It's rich in ...**
➔ Magnesium, which boosts immunity and helps promote relaxation and normal sleep patterns
➔ Fiber, balancing blood sugar levels and aiding healthy appetite and digestion
➔ Vitamin $B_6$, which encourages healthy iron levels in the body, thus improving energy levels, while also helping to keep the brain functioning optimally
➔ Healthy proteins, boosting alertness and performance

**Use in ...** sandwiches instead of mayonnaise; guacamole; add to salads; spread on toast instead of butter; make an avocado dressing to top a salad; blend with vanilla extract, yogurt with live cultures and honey for a nutritious smoothie.

SEE: SMOKED SALMON & AVOCADO CORNETS, P. 56; MISO BROTH WITH SHRIMP, P. 72; SALAD NIÇOISE WITH ARTICHOKES & ASPARAGUS, P. 80; WARM RAINBOW SALAD, P. 84

## Dark chocolate

✔ Reduces stress levels
✔ Lifts mood
✔ Improves alertness
✔ Encourages relaxation
✔ Raises serotonin levels
✔ Reduces pain and symptoms of stress

Dark chocolate is rich in a variety of nutrients and chemicals that work directly on the neurotransmitters in your brain to boost mood, alertness, and relaxation, while reducing pain and many of the symptoms of stress. Countless studies point to its ability to encourage a sense of well-being, and this is one ingredient that should be on the menu of anyone hoping to become happier.

**It's rich in ...**
➔ Flavonoids and other nutrients that have been shown to reduce stress hormones in the bloodstream
➔ Phenylethylamine, which causes changes in blood pressure and blood sugar levels, leading to increased alertness and excitement
➔ Theobromine, which enhances physical and mental relaxation
➔ Chemicals that prompt the release of endorphins, the body's pain-relieving and pleasure-promoting hormones, and serotonin, the antidepressant hormone

**Use in ...** spicy chiles and curries for a deeper flavor; melt and blend with a banana and yogurt with live cultures for a rich, nutritious smoothie; grate over oatmeal for an instant pick-me-up; add a handful of semisweet chocolate chips to baked goods; melt over fruit and nuts for a nourishing snack.

SEE: ICED BERRIES WITH DARK CHOCOLATE SAUCE, P. 112; DARK CHOCOLATE & RASPBERRY SOUFFLE, P. 114; CHOCOLATE-DIPPED FRUIT, P. 124

# Yogurt with live cultures

✔ Reduces stress hormones
✔ Helps ease anxiety and depression
✔ Encourages healthy digestion
✔ Boosts immunity
✔ Promotes relaxation
✔ Improves energy levels

A study found that the probiotics (healthy bacteria) contained in yogurt with live active cultures may alter brain chemistry and can help in the treatment of anxiety and depression-related disorders. It also helps lower stress hormones in the bloodstream.

### It's rich in ...

→ Calcium, which can encourage a healthy nervous system as well as restful sleep
→ Probiotics, which improve immunity and ease symptoms of depression and anxiety
→ Iodine, which boosts the production of thyroid hormones to encourage healthy energy levels and metabolism
→ Vitamin $B_{12}$, which is required for the production of oxygen-carrying red blood cells and the health of the nervous system

Use in ... breakfast cereals and muesli instead of milk; as a base for fruit smoothies to slow down the transit of fruit sugars in the blood; on sandwiches instead of mayonnaise; mix with lemon zest and herbs as a salad dressing; blend with a little vanilla sugar as an accompaniment for crisps, cakes, and other baked goods.

SEE: MUESLI WITH PEACHES & YOGURT, P. 38; BANANA OAT SMOOTHIE, P. 39; NUTTY PASSION FRUIT YOGURT, P. 40; APPLE & CRANBERRY GRANOLA P. 42; BRAZIL NUT & BANANA PARFAIT, P. 110; ICED BERRIES WITH DARK CHOCOLATE SAUCE, P. 112; FIG & GRAPE TARTS, P. 120

# Oats

✔ Nourish the nervous system
✔ Ease anxiety
✔ Balance blood sugar levels
✔ Encourage calm
✔ Boost libido
✔ Enhance memory and energy levels

Oats are renowned for their ability to encourage the health of the nervous system, and they have long been considered a "nervine" tonic. They are rich in fiber and slow-release carbohydrates that can help balance blood sugar levels and stabilize mood. Oats also contain healthy fatty acids that promote overall well-being.

### They are rich in ...

→ Slow-release carbohydrates, which are associated with the production of the mood-enhancing neurotransmitter serotonin
→ The B vitamins, encouraging the health of the nervous system
→ Soluble and insoluble fiber, helping to improve digestive health and the absorption of nutrients from food and to balance blood sugar
→ Zinc, which is required for healthy immunity, libido, hormone balance, energy levels, and memory

Use in ... homemade muesli and baked breakfast goods; as a topping for crisps and sweet and savory pies; as a coating for baked fish or chicken; in homemade soda bread.

SEE: MUESLI WITH PEACHES & YOGURT, P. 38; BANANA OAT SMOOTHIE, P. 39; APPLE & CRANBERRY GRANOLA, P. 42; FIG & APRICOT OAT BARS, P. 58; MACKEREL FILLETS WITH OAT TOPPING, P. 90; BRAZIL NUT & BANANA PARFAIT, P. 110

# Bananas

✔ Lift mood
✔ Encourage calm
✔ Raise serotonin levels
✔ Boost energy
✔ Enhance digestion
✔ Aid restful sleep
✔ Increase alertness

Bananas are one of the most nutritious fruits. The high levels of potassium nourish the nervous system, while helping to ensure a good supply of oxygenated blood to the brain. High levels of vitamin $B_6$ make bananas ideal for treating menstrual-related depression.

### They are rich in ...

→ Tryptophan, which encourages the production of serotonin, raising mood, facilitating relaxation and deep, restful sleep
→ Potassium, which boosts alertness and concentration, and lifts mood
→ Vitamin $B_6$, which aids the production of norepinephrine, a neurotransmitter that stimulates brain activity and enhances alertness and concentration, while helping to produce serotonin
→ Fiber, which encourages blood sugar balance and aid digestion

**Use in ...** pancakes or add to French-style crepes for a nutritious breakfast; keep a few bananas in the freezer and add to yogurt with live cultures, honey, or fresh fruit for an instant iced smoothie; bake alongside pork instead of apples; bake with brown sugar or honey for a warm dessert.

SEE: BANANA OAT SMOOTHIE, P. 39; STRAWBERRY & BANANA MUFFINS, P. 59; BANANA SUNFLOWER SEED COOKIES, P. 62; BRAZIL NUT & BANANA PARFAIT, P. 110

## Strawberries

- ✔ Balance moods
- ✔ Aid concentration
- ✔ Encourage digestion
- ✔ Help ease symptoms of PMS and seasonal affective disorder (SAD)
- ✔ Boost vitality and virility
- ✔ Raise energy levels

Like all berries, strawberries are rich in antioxidants, which have a host of beneficial effects on overall health and well-being, including boosting energy levels and protecting the brain from the effects of stress. Their high fiber levels promote efficient digestion and absorption of nutrients. As an excellent source of vitamin C, they improve immunity, too.

**They are rich in ...**

- → Manganese, for a healthy nervous system and energy production
- → Anthocyanins, powerful antioxidants that improve health on all levels and protect against many different degenerative diseases
- → Phenols, which have anti-inflammatory benefits to ease aches and pains
- → The B vitamins, encouraging a healthy nervous system and balanced moods

**Use in ...** smoothies; sprinkle on breakfast cereal and muesli; freeze and dip in dark chocolate sauce for a frosty, delicious treat; add to muffins, sweet breads, and other baked goods for moisture and added nutrients; puree and set with a little gelatin for a nutritious fruit gelatin; add to green salads with goat cheese and toasted walnuts.

**SEE: STRAWBERRY, WATERMELON & MINT SMOOTHIE, P. 36; STRAWBERRY & BANANA MUFFINS, P. 59; ICED BERRIES WITH DARK CHOCOLATE SAUCE, P. 112**

## Kale

- ✔ Boosts immunity
- ✔ Encourages brain health
- ✔ Enhances digestion
- ✔ Raises energy levels
- ✔ Stimulates detoxification and liver health, thus balancing hormones

Kale contains more than 13 times the daily recommended intake of vitamin K, a nutrient required for a healthy nervous system and brain function. A host of antioxidants provide support for your immune system and act as anti-inflammatories, easing aches and pains.

**It's rich in ...**

- → Iron, encouraging the production of red blood cells, which carry oxygen in the blood
- → Vitamin C, boosting immunity to help prevent damage to cells as a result of stress, and encouraging a healthy metabolism
- → Calcium, potassium, and vitamin A, essential for a healthy nervous system
- → Manganese, for energy production

**Use in ...** salads with a little red onion, red bell peppers, and golden raisins; braise with apples and top with walnuts and a sprinkling of cinnamon; stir into soups, stews, and casseroles; steam and top with lemon zest, sea salt, and olive oil; add to whole-wheat pasta with a light pesto and a good grating of Parmesan cheese.

**SEE: MINTED KALE SOUP, P. 68; THAI TURKEY BURGERS WITH CRISPY KALE, P. 98**

## Brazil nuts

✔ Balance hormones
✔ Improve energy levels
✔ Ease mood swings and lift mood
✔ Reduce anxiety

High in healthy monounsaturated fats, brazil nuts contain extremely high levels of selenium, a mineral known for its anti-anxiety, mood-lifting properties. Just three brazil nuts each day have been shown to increase levels of this nutrient significantly, affecting emotional health.

**They are rich in ...**
→ Selenium, which helps to balance mood and prevent anxiety and depression
→ Zinc, which is required for hormone balance, energy levels, and memory
→ Magnesium, aiding restful sleep and promoting healthy relaxation
→ The B vitamins, required for metabolism and to eliminate symptoms of fatigue, depression, and nervous disorders

**Use in ...** salads with feta cheese, grapes, and mixed salad greens; dip into dark chocolate for a mood-lifting snack; chop and add to muffins, chocolate brownies, cookies, and sweet breads; make a pesto with ground brazil nuts, lemon juice and zest, fresh tarragon, olive oil, and Parmesan cheese.

SEE: NUTTY PASSION FRUIT YOGURT, P. 40;
APPLE & CRANBERRY GRANOLA, P. 42;
BRAZIL NUT & BANANA PARFAIT, P. 110

## Peanuts

✔ Balance blood sugar
✔ Encourage serotonin production
✔ Promote restful sleep
✔ Boost memory
✔ Help symptoms of PMS and postnatal depression
✔ Help prevent overeating

Peanuts are a great source of healthy monounsaturated fats, as well as vitamin E, niacin, folic acid, and good-quality protein. They are as rich in antioxidants as many fruits and, with a low-GI rating, can help to balance blood sugar levels.

**They are rich in ...**
→ Vitamin $B_3$, which promotes normal brain functioning and boosts memory power
→ Tryptophan, which is essential for the production of serotonin, a key element in mood regulation and healthy sleep
→ Folic acid, encouraging a healthy nervous system
→ Manganese, which can help reduce symptoms of PMS and postnatal depression, while regulating neurotransmitters norepinephrine and serotonin

**Use in ...** salads with crunchy fresh vegetables; add to Asian curries, stir-fries, and noodle salads; spread peanut butter on whole-wheat breakfast toast or rice cakes, or just eat a spoonful of peanut butter as a midafternoon snack; try peanut butter and banana sandwiches, instead of jelly.

SEE: TURKEY & PEANUT NOODLE SALAD, P. 78;
CHICKEN & PEANUT STEW WITH BROWN RICE, P. 94

# Sesame seeds

✔ Antidepressant effect
✔ Balance blood sugar
✔ Regulate hormone production
✔ Encourage production of serotonin
✔ Reduce anxiety
✔ Reduce symptoms of PMS

Sesame seeds are incredibly rich in calcium and magnesium, both of which help to promote a healthy nervous system, relaxation, and restful sleep. They lower glucose levels in the blood, thus balancing blood sugar, and provide a dose of tryptophan, which helps sleep and mood.

### They are rich in ...
→ Sesamol, a chemical found to have antidepressant effects in cases of chronic stress
→ Vitamin $B_6$, helping to combat the symptoms of PMS, support the nervous system, and encourage relaxation
→ Zinc, which helps to prevent damage caused by stress
→ Vitamin $B_1$, which has calming properties and aids nerve function

**Use in ...** Asian salads; any type of hummus, including chickpea, lima bean, and edamame (soybean) versions; use sesame oil in stir-fries and salad dressings; add to cookies, oat bars, and other baked goods for mood-boosting snacks; try the darker seeds (black, brown, and red) to add flavor to curries and other Indian dishes.

SEE: SESAME SNAPS, P. 55; FIG & APRICOT OAT BARS, P. 58; SESAME-CRUSTED SALMON, P. 88; ORANGE, GINGER & SESAME RICE PUDDING, P. 122

# Eggs

✔ Regulate mood
✔ Encourage concentration and alertness
✔ Support the adrenal glands, which release stress hormones
✔ Boost energy levels
✔ Stabilize blood sugar
✔ Promote the release of serotonin

Eggs are a rich source of healthy proteins, which not only balance blood sugar and stabilize appetite, but also provide a wealth of amino acids that lift mood and help to facilitate restful sleep. They're particularly useful for symptoms associated with stress.

### They are rich in ...
→ Tryptophan, encouraging the release of the brain neurotransmitter serotonin, which lifts mood and helps to establish healthy sleep patterns
→ Choline, necessary for a healthy brain and nervous system, improving both memory and mood
→ Selenium, the antidepressant mineral that also helps to boost immunity and balance mood
→ Iodine, encouraging the health of the thyroid gland, which is responsible for energy levels and metabolism

**Use in ...** herbed omelets with spinach and mushrooms; try eggs scrambled with chives and topped with smoked haddock; eat hard-boiled eggs stuffed with yogurt with live culture, chives, and dill for a healthy snack; chop and add to salads; scramble and serve in a whole-wheat tortilla with fresh salsa, guacamole, and black beans.

SEE: BAKED EGGS WITH SPINACH, P. 43; POTATO & CORN HASH WITH FRAZZLED EGGS, P. 46

# Whole-wheat

✔ Promotes healthy digestion
✔ Balances blood sugar levels
✔ Promotes the release of serotonin
✔ Reduces symptoms of PMS
  and postnatal depression
✔ Encourages a balanced weight

Rich in tryptophan, which encourages the release of serotonin, and an excellent source of fiber and a little protein, whole-wheat is an excellent addition to a mood-boosting diet. It has high levels of the B vitamins, which support the nervous system, and also contains antioxidants that protect the body from stress-related damage.

**It's rich in ...**
→ Complex carbohydrates, which balance blood sugar and lift mood, aiding the production of serotonin
→ Manganese, reducing the symptoms of PMS and postnatal depression, while regulating the neurotransmitters norepinephrine and serotonin
→ Fiber, which balances blood sugar levels, promotes healthy digestion, and encourages healthy absorption of nutrients from food
→ Betaine, which reduces inflammation and associated aches and pains

**Use in ...** whole-wheat pastas with light vegetable sauces; try wheat berries (available from health food stores) in place of quinoa or rice in filling salads; sprinkle grains over soups, stews, and casseroles; serve whole-wheat tortillas or pita breads with hummus or peanut butter.

SEE: WHITE BEAN HUMMUS WITH PITA BITES, P. 50; THAI TURKEY BURGERS WITH CRISPY KALE, P. 98; PENNE WITH TOMATO, ARTICHOKE & OLIVE SAUCE, P. 104

# Garlic

✔ Boosts immunity
✔ Helps produce serotonin
✔ Lifts mood
✔ Supports the nervous system
✔ Encourages digestion and
  reduces bloating
✔ Increases energy levels
✔ Reduces fatigue
✔ Eases anxiety
✔ Promotes well-being

A recent German study found that raw garlic not only elevated the mood of the study participants, but also reduced fatigue, anxiety, and irritability. Garlic has also been used in the treatment of addictions, and is great for boosting the immune system.

**It's rich in ...**
→ Vitamin $B_6$, which encourages healthy iron levels, improving energy levels and maintaining optimal brain function.
→ Manganese, for a healthy nervous system
→ Selenium, vitamin C, and calcium, all of which have antidepressant effects and promote relaxation and well-being
→ Tryptophan, which is the amino acid responsible for promoting restful sleep and the production of the neurotransmitter serotonin

**Use in ...** anything! Crush raw cloves and add to salad dressings, stews, dips, casseroles, and soups; roast and spread on whole-wheat bread; use to flavor curries and pasta sauces; crush, add to a little mayonnaise flavored with the juice and peel of one lemon; stuff inside poultry when roasting, and mash into the gravy.

SEE: ROASTED GARLIC CROSTINI, P. 54; TURKEY SOUP WITH LEMON & BARLEY, P. 69; SQUASH, CHICKPEA & SWEET POTATO TAGINE, P. 106

# Asparagus

✔ Balances blood sugar
✔ Reduces irritability
✔ Increases libido
✔ Encourages healthy digestion
✔ Supports the nervous system
✔ Increases energy levels
✔ Improves immunity

Asparagus is one of the richest sources of rutin (a natural substance found in plants), which, along with vitamin C, can help to protect the body from infections by stimulating the immune system. It also contains a chemical that balances insulin levels, evening out blood sugar levels, and, through that, mood swings and irritability.

## It's rich in ...

→ Vitamin K, which is required for a healthy nervous system and brain function
→ Folic acid, reducing inflammation and supporting the nervous system
→ Prebiotics, which encourage the growth of immune-busting, digestion-enhancing probiotics in the digestive tract
→ The B vitamins, encouraging the health of the nervous system, promoting healthy metabolism and energy levels, and balancing blood sugar levels

**Use in ...** salads; stir into risottos and primavera pasta sauces; steam and serve with a little lemon and sea salt; roast with lemon zest and olive oil; steam and wrap with prosciutto or smoked salmon for a quick snack; sauté with tofu or chicken; steam and add to omelets with wild mushrooms or goat cheese.

SEE: SALAD NIÇOISE WITH ARTICHOKES & ASPARAGUS, P. 80; GINGER SCALLOPS WITH ASPARAGUS, P. 85

# Watermelon

- ✔ Boosts immunity
- ✔ Eases headaches and irritability
- ✔ Relaxes blood vessels
- ✔ Reduces fatigue
- ✔ Encourages healthy sleep patterns
- ✔ Encourages alertness

The flesh, peel, and seeds of this delicious, juicy fruit can be eaten to provide a wealth of key vitamins and minerals that support health on all levels. It was traditionally used to lift depression and to balance hormones, and its high antioxidant content encourages immunity.

### It's rich in ...

- → Water and natural electrolytes, which rehydrate, ease headaches, reduce irritability, and increase energy levels
- → Calcium, nourishing the nervous system and promoting restful sleep
- → Vitamins $B_1$ and $B_6$, balancing hormones and encouraging nerve transmission throughout the body
- → Potassium, for brain health and increased alertness

**Use in ...** salads, topped with feta cheese and toasted pecans; blend in smoothies with a little yogurt with live cultures and a few sprigs of mint; puree with kiwi, mint, orange peel, and yellow melon and serve as a refreshing cold soup.

SEE: STRAWBERRY, WATERMELON & MINT SMOOTHIE, P. 36; WATERMELON, GINGER & LIME GRANITA, P. 108; TROPICAL FRUIT SALAD WITH GREEN TEA SYRUP, P. 121

# Ginger

✔ Stimulates digestion
✔ Eases nausea
✔ Reduces muscle pain and headaches
✔ Lifts mood
✔ Encourages a sense of calm
✔ Stimulates the taste buds
✔ Regulates blood sugar levels

In traditional Chinese medicine, ginger has been used for centuries in the treatment of depression and other emotional problems. Various studies performed in the last few years have verified the fact that it is calming and, in some cases, mimics the action of antidepressants. Its warming qualities also make it useful for aches and pains.

### It's rich in ...

➜ The amino acid phenylalanine, which reduces pain, controls appetite, encourages alertness, and improves memory
➜ Threonine, an amino acid that boosts immunity and minimizes inflammation
➜ Tryptophan, encouraging restful sleep and stable moods
➜ Gingerol, an anti-inflammatory agent that eases nausea, promotes healthy digestion, and eases pain

**Use in ...** lemon and ginger tea, first thing in the morning to stimulate digestion; grate into curries, soups, stews, and casseroles; use in Asian salads and stir-fries; stew with rhubarb for a delicious compote; stir into chocolate dishes and baked goods for extra flavor.

SEE: GINGER SCALLOPS WITH ASPARAGUS, P. 85; CHICKEN & PEANUT STEW WITH BROWN RICE, P. 94; CAULIFLOWER & TURKEY BIRYANI, P. 96; TURKEY, LENTIL & APRICOT STEW, P. 97; THAI BEEF & MIXED PEPPER STIR-FRY, P. 100

# Figs

✔ Encourage brain and nervous system health
✔ Balance blood sugar
✔ Boost libido
✔ Enhance immunity
✔ Reduce inflammation and pain
✔ Balance hormones
✔ Improve liver health

Figs are an excellent source of vitamins, minerals, and trace elements, encouraging health on all levels, as well as controlling blood pressure, easing muscular aches, and encouraging healthy brain function.

### They are rich in ...

➜ Omega-3 and omega-6 oils, preventing inflammation and related pain, building muscle and tissue, and enhancing normal brain function
➜ Potassium, regulating blood sugar levels, preventing cramping, boosting immunity, and encouraging the health of the heart and nervous system
➜ Amino acids, such as arginine, which encourage libido
➜ Soluble and insoluble fiber, encouraging digestion, balancing blood sugar, and mopping up toxins to improve liver health and, therefore, hormone balance

**Use in ...** fruitcakes and pies; chop and add to breakfast cereals and muesli; roast and puree into a compote to serve with yogurt with live cultures; serve with creamy blue cheese and walnuts on a bed of lettuce for a filling salad; marinate in balsamic vinegar and lemon juice and serve with mozzarella balls and pecans.

SEE: FIG & APRICOT OAT BARS, P. 58; BAKED FIGS WITH MASCARPONE, P. 113; FIG, RASPBERRY & PROSCIUTTO SALAD, P. 74

# Barley

✔ Balances blood sugar
✔ Encourages digestion
✔ Boosts energy levels
✔ Encourages balanced weight
✔ Reduces anxiety
✔ Helps prevent depression
✔ Lifts mood

Barley is one of the oldest cultivated grains and, as a whole grain, is rich in fiber, selenium, and the B vitamins, all of which play a role in balancing mood. In fact, one cup of barley contains more than half of your daily selenium requirement. The manganese it contains helps to provide an overall sense of well-being.

## It's rich in ...

→ Tryptophan, an amino acid that stimulates the production of the feel-good chemical serotonin and encourages restful sleep
→ Copper, promoting the uptake of iron to boost energy levels
→ Beta-glucan, a chemical that balances blood sugar levels and improves the body's response to glucose
→ Selenium, which helps to balance moods and prevent anxiety and depression

**Use in ...** risottos, pilafs, and puddings instead of rice; barley water, with fresh lemon juice to stimulate digestion and encourage calm; bulk out soups, stews, and casseroles with barley to add healthy proteins, slow-release carbs, and flavor; stuff into bell peppers with onions, pine nuts, and feta cheese.

SEE: TURKEY SOUP WITH LEMON & BARLEY, P. 69

# Lentils

✔ Balance blood sugar
✔ Promote healthy digestion
✔ Ease anxiety
✔ Reduce symptoms of depression
✔ Encourage the release of serotonin
✔ Raise energy levels
✔ Aid restful sleep

Lentils are a supremely nutritious member of the legume family, with excellent levels of fiber, which control blood sugar, and folic acid, which supports a healthy nervous system. A good source of protein, lentils contain many amino acids that encourage a sense of well-being and actively work to reduce symptoms of depression.

## They are rich in ...

→ Soluble fiber, helping to stabilize blood sugar levels, while providing a steady source of energy
→ Iron, producing hemoglobin, which is necessary for a good supply of oxygenated blood
→ Tryptophan in high quantities, which encourages the release of serotonin, thereby lifting mood and helping sleep
→ Magnesium, the "antistress" mineral that decreases the release of the stress hormone cortisol

**Use in ...** soups, stews, casseroles, and curries; serve cool or warm as a salad, with goat cheese and lemon juice; use instead of rice as a bed for fish, curries, and stews; use in dhal, a nutrient-rich Indian dish; braise with chile and oranges.

SEE: LENTIL & PEA SOUP, P. 66; TURKEY, LENTIL & APRICOT STEW, P. 97

# Artichokes

✔ Encourage digestion
✔ Improve health of the nervous system
✔ Enhance metabolism
✔ Help restore healthy brain function
✔ Boost immunity
✔ Reduce symptoms of stress
✔ Ease irritability
✔ Promote hormone balance

Antioxidant-rich artichokes are brimming with nutrients to help lift mood and keep the symptoms of depression at bay. A rich source of minerals, such as copper, calcium, iron, and potassium, they naturally boost energy levels while protecting the liver, thus encouraging hormonal balance.

**They are rich in ...**

➔ Vitamin K, for a healthy nervous system and brain function
➔ Vitamin C, helping to balance the stress hormone cortisol in the body, boost immunity, and ease digestion
➔ Inulin, a prebiotic that stimulates the growth of healthy bacteria in the digestive tract, thereby aiding digestion and encouraging healthy elimination
➔ Calcium, which eases anxiety and restores nervous system function

**Use in ...** salads, with roasted vegetables; use jars of marinated artichokes in pasta sauces, antipasti plates, and Mediterranean salads; in sandwiches, with basil, pesto, and mozzarella cheese; steam and serve with lemon butter or lemon-flavored yogurt; cook with mussels or use as a base for vegetable terrines.

SEE: SALAD NIÇOISE WITH ARTICHOKES & ASPARAGUS, P. 80; HERBED ARTICHOKE CASSEROLE, P. 102; PENNE WITH TOMATO, ARTICHOKE & OLIVE SAUCE, P. 104

# Grapes

✔ Lift mood
✔ Improve concentration
✔ Increase serotonin levels
✔ Enhance oxygen flow to the brain
✔ Boost immunity
✔ Encourage healthy digestion
✔ Reduce inflammation

Grapes are full of essential vitamins, minerals, and trace elements. In particular, resveratrol, found in the seeds and skin of grapes, has been shown to increase blood flow to the brain, improve concentration, and promote higher levels of antidepressant chemicals serotonin and noradrenaline.

**They are rich in ...**

➔ Manganese, a component in nerve health and required for thyroid hormone production, low levels of which can lower mood
➔ Vitamin K, improving brain function and promoting a healthy nervous system
➔ Fiber and slow-release carbs, for better blood sugar balance, better insulin regulation, and increased insulin sensitivity
➔ Phytonutrients, such as flavonoids and resveratrol, encouraging healthy digestion and immunity, and aiding concentration

**Use in ...** salads, with feta cheese and almonds; use frozen, as a snack to keep blood sugar levels balanced; in fruit tarts; alongside berries and bananas in nourishing smoothies; braise with chicken and walnuts; serve in a creamy sauce with sole for Sole Véronique.

SEE: BEET, GRAPE & FETA SALAD, P. 79; FIG & GRAPE TARTS, P. 120; TROPICAL FRUIT SALAD WITH GREEN TEA SYRUP, P. 121

# WHAT'S YOUR PROBLEM?

The functional foods on the following pages work to heal specific parts of your mind and body, targeting and relieving the symptoms of depression. Decide which symptoms affect you and choose from the foods and recipes that help combat them. These icons are used throughout the recipe section to highlight which recipes offer the most effective treatment.

### Low mood

Brazil nuts, spinach, oranges, grapefruit, herring, brown rice, spelt, edamame (soybeans), kidney beans, crab, turkey, green tea, kale, apricots, almonds, blueberries, dark chocolate, grapes, asparagus, ginger, barley, garlic, mackerel, sesame seeds, bananas, sunflower seeds.

**Recipes Include:**
Mackerel pâté on rye crisps, p. 52; Orange, ginger & sesame rice pudding, p. 122

### Addictions

Kale, cabbage, romaine lettuce, beet, carrots, berries, grapefruit, ginger, eggs, brazil nuts, turkey, dark chocolate, peppermint, mackerel, cod, chickpeas, rye, strawberries.

**Recipes Include:**
Potato & corn hash with frazzled eggs, p. 46; Rare beef & baby beet salad, p. 76; Warm rainbow salad, p. 84; Turkey, lentil & apricot stew, p. 97

### Anxiety

Peaches, blueberries, almonds, oats, dark chocolate, salmon, broccoli, brown rice, kelp/seaweed, milk, turkey, melon, beef, peanuts, edamame (soybeans), grapefruit, cherries, romaine lettuce, barley, ginger, garlic, sesame seeds, brazil nuts.

**Recipes Include:**
Muesli with peaches & yogurt, p. 38; Broccoli & almond soup, p. 70; Tomato, tofu & hot pepper salad, p. 82

### Irritability

Tuna, salmon, mackerel, oats, black beans, pumpkin seeds, artichokes, dark chocolate, spinach, bananas, peanuts, brown rice, cashew nuts, cabbage, edamame (soybeans), cod, sunflower seeds, asparagus, figs, watermelon, garlic, brazil nuts.

**Recipes Include:**
Salad niçoise with artichokes & asparagus, p. 80; Herbed artichoke casserole, p. 102

### Fatigue

Hazelnuts, yogurt with live cultures, sesame seeds, spinach, chickpeas, cocoa, pomegranate, figs, eggs, kale, beet, apricots, coconut, cranberries, dates, olives, cinnamon, salmon, brazil nuts, black currants, watermelon, asparagus, garlic, mackerel, lentils.
**Recipes Include:**
Nutty passion fruit yogurt, p. 40; Baked eggs with spinach, p. 43; Olive & sun-dried tomato biscuits, p. 65

### Depression

Whole grains, oats, nuts, seeds, beans, brown rice, brewer's yeast (or Marmite), quinoa, cabbage, brazil nuts, dark chocolate, sweet potatoes, kiwi, bell peppers, oranges, carrots, melon, apricots, grapes, artichokes, barley, garlic, turkey, mackerel, lentils, sesame seeds, bananas, sunflower seeds, salmon.
**Recipes Include:**
Banana & sunflower seed cookies, p. 62; Chocolate-dipped fruit, p. 124

### PMS

Sunflower seeds, dairy produce, bananas, oranges, wheat germ, salmon, sesame seeds, black beans, yogurt with live cultures, mackerel, tomatoes, cranberries, barley, strawberries, tuna, blueberries, oats, watermelon, kale, artichokes, spinach, brazil nuts.
**Recipes Include:**
Sesame seed snaps, p. 55; Minted kale soup, p. 68; Watermelon, ginger & lime granita, p. 108

### Poor concentration

Dark chocolate, oranges, pecans, walnuts, rosemary, avocado, spelt, quinoa, popcorn, blueberries, eggs, dairy produce, spinach, squash, potatoes, mango, asparagus, strawberries, watermelon, grapes, artichokes, ginger.
**Recipes Include:**
Eggs Benedict with smoked salmon, p. 44; Smoked salmon & avocado cornets, p. 56; Fig & grape tarts, p. 120

## Overeating

Chicken, edamame (soybeans), eggs, chickpeas, black beans, lentils, rye, whole wheat, dark chocolate, walnuts, almonds, peanuts, yogurt with live cultures, salmon, popcorn, coconut, apple cider vinegar, figs.

**Recipes Include:**
Roasted garlic crostini, p. 54; Chicken & peanut stew with brown rice, p. 94; Herbed artichoke casserole, p. 102; Dark chocolate & raspberry soufflé, p. 114

## Mood swings

Whole grains, beans, tuna, salmon, halibut, cheese, yogurt, green tea, dark chocolate, mushrooms, almonds, brazil nuts, pistachios, blueberries, pomegranate, cinnamon, leafy green vegetables, watermelon, ginger, barley, garlic.

**Recipes Include:**
Blueberry & mint smoothie, p. 60; Turkey soup with lemon & barley, p. 69; Sesame-crusted salmon, p. 88

## Aches & pains

Salmon, ginger, cherries, olive oil, green tea, walnuts, flaxseed, edamame (soybeans), turmeric, grapes, sage, spelt, quinoa, rye, cocoa, brazil nuts, oats, apricots, avocado, bananas, fava beans, garlic, butternut squash, sweet potatoes.

**Recipes Include:**
Cherry & nectarine meringe, p. 118; Stir-fried tofu with shrimp & rice noodles, p. 91; Brazil nut & banana parfait, p. 110

## Winter blues

Salmon, mackerel, almonds, eggs, kale, sweet potatoes, brazil nuts, turkey, dark chocolate, oats, strawberries, avocado, Romaine lettuce, bananas, dairy produce, pineapple, sour cherries, barley, garlic, lentils, sesame seeds.

**Recipes Include:**
Mackerel pâté on rye crisps, p. 52; Smoked salmon & avocado cornets, p. 56; Turkey soup with lemon & barley, p. 69; Brazil nut & banana parfait, p. 110

## Lack of desire

Celery, shellfish, pineapple, bananas, avocado, almonds, mango, peaches, strawberries, eggs, figs, garlic, dark chocolate, cocoa, chile peppers, honey, pumpkin seeds, asparagus.
**Recipes Include:**
Zucchini & Stilton fritters, p. 47; Fig & apricot oat bars, p. 58; Miso broth with shrimp, p. 72; Ginger scallops with asparagus, p. 85

## Low self-esteem

Blueberries, carrots, butternut squash, tomatoes, kale, spinach, romaine lettuce, alfalfa, cherries, grapes, tuna, salmon, almonds, dates, rye, chickpeas, lentils, broccoli, mackerel.
**Recipes Include:**
Butternut squash & ricotta frittata, p. 48; Broccoli & almond soup, p. 70; Beet, grape & feta salad, p. 79; Mackerel & asparagus tart, p. 86

## Sleep problems

Turkey, bananas, potatoes, honey, oats, almonds, flaxseed, sunflower seeds, cherries, tuna, peanuts, cheese, yogurt with live cultures, brown rice, lentils, quinoa, dates, mango, watermelon, ginger, barley, garlic, brazil nuts.
**Recipes Include:**
Potato & corn hash with frazzled eggs, p. 46; Sesame snaps, p. 55; Goat cheese, apple & broccoli salad, p. 73; Turkey & peanut noodle salad, p. 78

## Postnatal blues

Avocado, coconut, flaxseed, apples, rye, whole wheat, oats, strawberries, pumpkin seeds, dairy produce, brown rice, sweet potatoes, lentils, dark chocolate, blueberries, eggs, brazil nuts, kidney beans, sesame seeds, watermelon, artichokes, sunflower seeds.
**Recipes Include:**
Strawberry, watermelon & mint smoothie, p. 36; Lentil & pea soup, p. 66

# PUTTING IT
# ALL TOGETHER

| Meal Planner | Monday | Tuesday | Wednesday |
|---|---|---|---|
| **Breakfast** | Muesli with peaches & yogurt, p. 38 | Baked eggs with spinach, p. 43 | Apple & cranberry granola, p. 42 |
| **Morning snack** | Chocolate-covered brazil nuts | ½ avocado with 1 teaspoon lemon mayonnaise | Boiled egg |
| **Lunch** | Ginger scallops with asparagus, p. 85 | Beet, grape & feta salad, p. 79 | Tomato, tofu & hot pepper salad, p. 82 |
| **Afternoon snack** | Sesame snaps, p. 55 | Olive & sun-dried tomato biscuits, p. 64 | Chocolate-dipped fruit, p. 124 |
| **Dinner** | Cauliflower & turkey biriyani, p. 96 | Squash, chickpea & sweet potato tagine, p. 106 | Mackerel fillets with oat topping, p. 90 |
| **Dessert** | Baked figs with mascarpone, p. 113 | Dark chocolate & raspberry soufflé, p. 114 | Watermelon, ginger & lime granita, p 108 |

# WEEK 1

## Thursday

Pink grapefruit with maple syrup

Smoked salmon & avocado cornets, p. 56

Lentil & pea soup, p. 66

Strawberry & banana muffins, p. 59

Penne with tomato, artichoke & olive sauce, p. 104

Cherry & nectarine meringue, p. 118

## Friday

Nutty passion fruit yogurt, p. 40

Banana sunflower seed cookies, p. 62

Fig, raspberry & prosciutto salad, p. 74

Mackerel pâté on rye crisps, p. 52

Turkey, lentil & apricot stew, p. 97

Orange, ginger & sesame rice pudding, p. 122

## Saturday

Zucchini & Stilton fritters, p. 47

Fig & apricot oat bars, p. 58

Salad niçoise with artichokes & asparagus, p. 80

Roasted garlic crostini, p. 54

Creamy roasted peppers with mixed grains, p. 105

Tipsy blueberry & mascarpone desserts, p. 116

## Sunday

Eggs Benedict with smoked salmon, p. 44

Handful of almonds

Goat cheese, apple & broccoli salad, p. 73

White bean hummus with pita bites, p. 50

Chicken & peanut stew with brown rice, p. 94

Iced berries with dark chocolate sauce, p. 112

| Meal Planner | Monday | Tuesday | Wednesday |
| --- | --- | --- | --- |
| **Breakfast** | Apple & cranberry granola, p. 42 | Nutty passion fruit yogurt, p. 40 | Strawberry, watermelon & mint smoothie, p. 36 |
| **Morning snack** | Blueberry & mint smoothie, p. 60 | Mackerel pâté on rye crisps, p. 52 | Handful of grapes & Brie |
| **Lunch** | Miso broth with shrimp, p. 72 | Warm rainbow salad, p. 84 | Mackerel & asparagus tart, p. 86 |
| **Afternoon snack** | Chocolate-covered brazil nuts | Banana sunflower seed cookies, p. 62 | Roasted garlic crostini, p. 54 |
| **Dinner** | Herbed artichoke casserole, p. 102 | Sesame-crusted salmon, p. 88 | Stir-fried tofu with shrimp & rice noodles, p. 91 |
| **Dessert** | Tropical fruit salad with green tea syrup, p. 121 | Poached apricots with orange flower water, p. 125 | Brazil nut & banana parfait, p. 110 |

# WEEK 2

| Thursday | Friday | Saturday | Sunday |
|---|---|---|---|
| Banana oat smoothie, p. 39 | Baked eggs with spinach, p. 43 | Potato & corn hash with frazzled eggs, p. 46 | Butternut squash & ricotta frittata, p. 48 |
| Olive & sun-dried tomato biscuits, p. 64 | Sesame snaps, p. 55 | Smoked salmon & avocado cornets, p. 56 | Fig & apricot oat bars, p. 58 |
| Broccoli & almond soup, p. 70 | Rare beef & baby beet salad, p. 76 | Minted kale soup, p. 68 | Turkey soup with lemon & barley, p. 69 |
| ½ papaya | Blueberry & mint smoothie, p. 60 | Strawberry & banana muffins, p. 59 | White bean hummus with pitta bites, p. 50 |
| Thai turkey burgers with crispy kale, p. 98 | Red snapper with capers & warm tomato salad, p. 92 | Penne with tomato, artichoke & olive sauce, p. 104 | Thai beef & mixed pepper stir-fry, p. 100 |
| Watermelon, ginger & lime granita, p. 108 | Orange, ginger & sesame rice pudding, p. 122 | Chocolate-dipped fruit, p. 124 | Fig & grape tarts, p. 120 |

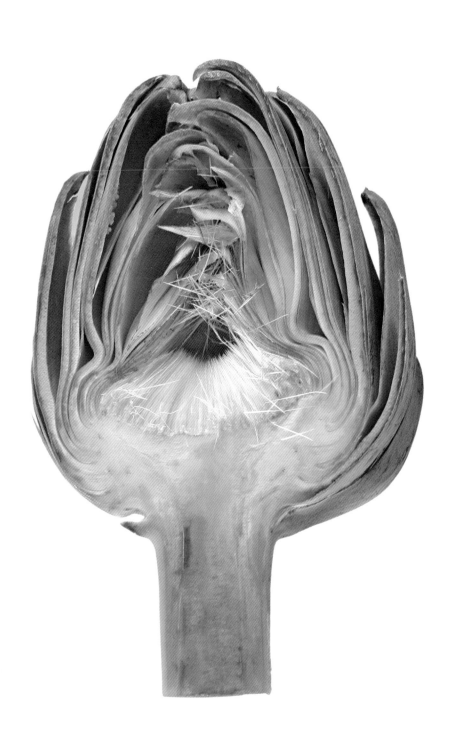

# HAPPY
# RECIPES

# STRAWBERRY, WATERMELON & MINT SMOOTHIE

This fresh-tasting, antioxidant-rich smoothie is perfect for a quick breakfast or nourishing snack.

**Preparation time:** 5 minutes
**Serves 4**

................

16 large **strawberries**, hulled
1 medium **watermelon**,
    peeled and seeded
3 tablespoons chopped **mint**
½ cup **papaya juice**

Place all the ingredients in a blender or food processor and blend until smooth. Divide among 4 tall glasses and serve immediately.

.............................................

In warm weather, add a few ice cubes or use frozen strawberries.

.............................................

# MUESLI WITH PEACHES & YOGURT

This sweet, satisfying muesli contains a host of anxiety-combating ingredients.

**Preparation time:** 15 minutes, plus soaking
**Cooking time:** 5 minutes (optional)
**Serves 4**
................

2 cups **rolled oats**
½ cup **wheat germ**
⅓ cup **sunflower seeds**
3 tablespoons **sesame seeds** or **flaxseed**
¼ cup **pumpkin seeds**
⅓ cup **almonds**
⅓ cup **hazelnuts**
½ cup chopped soft **dried apricots**
⅓ cup **dried cranberries**
⅓ cup **golden raisins**
1½ cups **peach** or **white grape juice**
1½ cups **Greek yogurt with live active cultures**
2 **peaches**, peeled, pitted, and sliced

Put the rolled oats into a large bowl and stir in the wheat germ, seeds, nuts, and dried fruits. Add the juice and let soak for at least 4 hours, or overnight.
...........................................................

When all of the juice has been absorbed, divide among 4 serving bowls and top with the yogurt and sliced peaches. Serve immediately.
...........................................

If you prefer a warm breakfast, transfer the soaked muesli to a saucepan and cook over low heat, stirring frequently, for about 5 minutes, until heated through. Serve with the yogurt and peaches.
.............................................

# BANANA OAT SMOOTHIE

This smoothie is unbelievably filling, perfect for a speedy breakfast before a busy day.

**Preparation time:** 5 minutes
**Serves 4**

.................

⅔ cup **steel-cut oats**
2 cups **plain yogurt with live active cultures**
4 **bananas**, coarsely chopped
2 cups **skim milk** or **rice milk**
3 tablespoons **honey**
1 teaspoon **ground cinnamon**

Place all the ingredients in a blender or food processor and blend until smooth, then divide among 4 large glasses to serve.

.............................................................

To vary the flavor from time to time, add a handful of pecans and substitute maple syrup for the honey.

.......................................

# NUTTY PASSION FRUIT YOGURT

This nutty, seed-rich yogurt will help to balance your moods and boost energy levels for the day ahead.

**Preparation time:** 10 minutes
**Serves 4**

seeds and pulp from 4 **passion fruit**
2 cups **plain yogurt with live active cultures**
½ cup **wild honey**
¾ cup toasted **hazelnuts**, coarsely chopped
⅓ cup **brazil nuts**, coarsely chopped
⅓ cup **sunflower seeds**
8 **clementines**, peeled and chopped

Place the passion fruit seeds and pulp into a large bowl. Add the yogurt and mix together gently.

Put 1 tablespoon of the honey in each of 4 narrow glasses and sprinkle with half the nuts and half the sunflower seeds. Spoon half the yogurt over the nuts and arrange half the clementine pieces on top.

Repeat the layering, reserving a few of the nuts for decoration. Sprinkle the nuts over the top and chill until ready to serve.

# APPLE & CRANBERRY GRANOLA

The oats in this tasty breakfast granola will get you going for the day and help to establish a feeling of calm.

**Preparation time:** 15 minutes
**Cooking time:** 15–30 minutes
**Serves 12**

2 large **apples**, peeled, cored, and chopped
¼ cup **maple syrup**
2 teaspoons **ground cinnamon**
2 tablespoons **olive oil**
1 teaspoon grated **nutmeg**
2¾ cups **rolled oats**
2 tablespoons **flaxseed**
⅓ cup **almonds**, crushed
⅓ cup **brazil nuts**, crushed
½ cup **pecan halves**, crushed
⅓ cup **sunflower seeds**
1 cup **dried cranberries**

**To serve**
½ cup **plain yogurt with live active cultures** per serving
handful of fresh fruit (**grapes, blueberries, or sliced peach**) per serving

Place the apples, maple syrup, cinnamon, olive oil, and nutmeg in a blender or food processor and blend until smooth.

Place the oats, flaxseed, almonds, brazil nuts, pecan nuts, and sunflower seeds in a large bowl, add the apple mixture, and stir until well coated.

Spread out on a lightly greased baking sheet and cook in a preheated oven, at 325°F, for 15–30 minutes, stirring frequently until it turns golden brown and no steam rises when you stir it. Remove from the oven, let cool, and stir in the cranberries.

The granola can be stored in an airtight container for up to 3 weeks. Serve topped with yogurt and fresh fruit.

# BAKED EGGS WITH SPINACH

This rich, delicious breakfast dish is bursting with nutrients and is ideal for a lazy weekend morning.

**Preparation time:** 15 minutes
**Cooking time:** 25 minutes
**Serves 4**
................

1 tablespoon **unsalted butter**,
  plus extra for greasing
½ **onion**, finely chopped
9 cups coarsely chopped **spinach**
  (about 1 lb), thawed if frozen
¼ cup **heavy cream** or **Greek yogurt with
  live active cultures**
½ teaspoon grated **nutmeg**
4 **eggs**
sea salt and **black pepper**

**To serve**
whole-wheat toast
unsmoked turkey bacon

Heat the butter in a large saucepan, add the onion, and cook over medium heat until just beginning to brown at the edges. Add the spinach and cook for 5 minutes, stirring frequently, until wilted. Remove from the heat and season to taste.
................

Divide the spinach mixture among 4 greased ramekins, about 3 inches in diameter. Drizzle the cream over the spinach, sprinkle with nutmeg, and top each ramekin with an egg, being careful to avoid break the yolks.
................

Season to taste and place in a preheated oven, at 400°F, for 12–15 minutes, or until the egg whites have just set. Serve with whole-wheat toast and unsmoked turkey bacon.
................

# EGGS BENEDICT WITH SMOKED SALMON

This is an excellent start to the day, stabilizing blood sugar, lifting your mood, and reducing stress hormones.

**Preparation time:** 10 minutes
**Cooking time:** 20 minutes
**Serves 4**

2 tablespoons **tarragon vinegar**
4 extra-large **eggs**
4 **whole-wheat English muffins**,
    split and toasted
8 small slices of **smoked salmon**
snipped **chives**, to garnish

**Tarragon hollandaise**
1 cup **plain yogurt with live active cultures**
3 **egg yolks**
2 teaspoons **lemon juice**
finely grated zest of ½ **lemon**
½ teaspoon **sea salt**
2 teaspoons finely chopped **tarragon**
½ teaspoon **Dijon mustard**
**black pepper**

To make the hollandaise sauce, put the yogurt, egg yolks, and lemon juice into a heatproof bowl, stir well, and set over a saucepan of gently simmering water, being careful to avoid letting the water touch the bottom of the bowl.

Stir vigorously for about 15 minutes, until the sauce heats and thickens. Stir in the lemon zest, salt, tarragon, and mustard, and season to taste with black pepper. Remove from the heat and set aside.

Bring a saucepan of water to a boil, add the vinegar, and reduce the heat to a slow simmer. One by one, crack the eggs into the water and cook for 3–4 minutes, or until the whites are firm but the yolks still runny.

Divide the toasted muffin halves among 4 serving plates and top with the salmon. Arrange the poached eggs on top and drizzle with the hollandaise sauce. Garnish with snipped chives and serve immediately.

# POTATO & CORN HASH WITH FRAZZLED EGGS

This dish will satisfy the heartiest appetite, sustaining energy and encouraging relaxation even at the most stressful times.

**Preparation time:** 15 minutes
**Cooking time:** 30 minutes
**Serves 4**

6 **red-skinned** or **white round potatoes**, peeled and diced
2 tablespoons **olive oil**
1 large **onion**, finely chopped
1 large **green bell pepper**, cored, seeded, and chopped
1 teaspoon **smoked paprika**
1¼ cups drained canned **corn kernels**
**olive oil** spray
4 extra-large **eggs**
2 tablespoons snipped **chives**
**sea salt** and **black pepper**

Cook the potatoes in a large saucepan of lightly salted boiling water for 12–15 minutes, until tender, then drain in a colander.

Meanwhile, heat the oil in a large nonstick, ovenproof skillet over medium heat. Add the onion and green bell pepper and cook, stirring occasionally, for 7–8 minutes, until softened and lightly golden brown.

Add the cooked potatoes, smoked paprika, and corn kernels, season generously, and cook for 3–4 minutes, stirring frequently. Slide the skillet under a preheated hot broiler, keeping the handle away from the heat, and broil for 2–3 minutes, until crispy.

Meanwhile, spray a large skillet with olive oil spray and place over medium heat until hot. Crack the eggs into the skillet and cook for 3 minutes, until the whites are set and crispy.

Serve the eggs immediately with the potato and corn hash, sprinkled with the chives.

# ZUCCHINI & STILTON FRITTERS

Rich in antioxidants and folic acid, these delicious fritters make a great breakfast or appetizer.

**Preparation time:** 10 minutes
**Cooking time:** 20 minutes
**Serves 4**

2 tablespoons **olive oil**
1 large **zucchini**, finely chopped
3 **eggs**
⅔ cup **milk**
1¼ cup **all-purpose flour**, sifted
1¼ teaspoons **baking powder**
2 cups drained, rinsed canned **great Northern beans**
handful of **parsley**, chopped
3 **scallions**, chopped
2 cups drained canned **corn kernels**
1 cup crumbled **Stilton** or **other blue cheese**
**sea salt** and **black pepper**
**poached eggs**, to serve

Heat half the oil in a nonstick skillet, add the zucchini, and sauté for 3–4 minutes, until golden brown and tender.

Beat together the eggs, milk, flour, and baking powder in a bowl, then stir in the beans, parsley, scallions, corn, Stilton, and the cooked zucchini. Season to taste.

Heat the remaining oil in the skillet and add tablespoons of the batter to the pan, a few at a time. Gently flatten each fritter with the back of a fork and cook for 1–2 minutes on each side, until golden.

Repeat with the remaining batter, keeping the cooked fritters warm in a low oven while you finish cooking the rest. Serve with poached eggs.

# BUTTERNUT SQUASH & RICOTTA FRITTATA

This filling, balancing frittata makes a nice weekend breakfast served with whole-wheat toast.

**Preparation time:** 10 minutes
**Cooking time:** 30 minutes
**Serves 4**

1 tablespoon **extra virgin canola oil**
1 red **onion**, thinly sliced
½ **butternut squash**, peeled and diced
8 **eggs**
1 tablespoon chopped **thyme**
2 tablespoons chopped **sage**
½ cup **ricotta cheese**
**sea salt** and **black pepper**
**whole-wheat toast**, to serve

Heat the oil in a large nonstick, ovenproof skillet over medium-low heat, and add the onion and butternut squash. Cover loosely and cook gently, stirring frequently, for 18–20 minutes or until tender and golden.

Beat the eggs lightly with the thyme, sage, and ricotta, then season generously and pour over the butternut squash. Cook for another 2–3 minutes, until the egg is almost set, stirring occasionally to prevent the bottom from burning.

Slide the pan under a preheated broiler, keeping the handle away from the heat, and broil for 3–4 minutes, or until the egg is set and the frittata is golden. Cut into wedges and serve with whole-wheat toast.

# WHITE BEAN HUMMUS WITH PITA BITES

This bean hummus makes a pleasant change from the traditional chickpeas and it's equally nutritious.

**Preparation time:** 10 minutes
**Serves 12**

1 (15 oz) can **cannellini** or **lima beans**
½ cup **tahini**
½ cup **lemon juice**
finely grated zest of 1 **lemon**
1 **garlic clove**, crushed
pinch of **sea salt**
2 tablespoons **olive oil**
2 tablespoons chopped **parsley** (optional)
1 **whole-wheat pita bread** per serving,
   toasted and cut into strips

Drain the beans, reserving 2 tablespoons of liquid from the can, and put into a blender or food processor with the tahini, lemon juice and zest, garlic, and salt. Blend until smooth, then, with the motor still running, add half the olive oil and a little of the reserved liquid if the mixture is too thick.

Transfer to a serving bowl and drizzle with the remaining olive oil. Sprinkle with the chopped parsley, if desired, and serve with toasted pita strips. The hummus can be stored in an airtight container in the refrigerator for up to 3 days.

# MACKEREL PÂTÉ ON RYE CRISPS

Bursting with brain-nourishing omega-3 oils, this delicious pâté is an excellent way to add fish to the diet.

**Preparation time:** 15 minutes
**Serves 4**
................

4 **smoked mackerel fillets,**
   skin and bones removed
¼ cup **cream cheese**
½ cup **mascarpone cheese**
½ cup **crème fraîche** or **Greek yogurt**
1 teaspoon chopped **dill**, plus extra
   to garnish
4 teaspoons hot **horseradish sauce**
finely grated zest and juice of 1 **lemon**
**black pepper**

**To serve**
4 thin slices of **dark rye bread**, toasted
**red endive** leaves

Place 3 of the mackerel fillets, the cream cheese, mascarpone, crème fraîche, dill, horseradish, and lemon zest in a blender or food processor and blend until smooth.
...................................................................

Transfer the mixture to a serving bowl, flake the remaining mackerel, and add to the bowl with the lemon juice. Season with black pepper and stir to combine.
...................................................................

Serve with rye toast and red endive leaves for scooping. The pâté can be stored in an airtight container in the refrigerator for up to 2 days.
...................................................................

# ROASTED GARLIC CROSTINI

Eat these crunchy garlicky bites plain or top with basil leaves, tomatoes, tapenade, avocado, or roasted peppers.

**Preparation time:** 10 minutes
**Cooking time:** 45 minutes
**Serves 4**

4 heads of **garlic**
¼ cup **olive oil**
1 teaspoon **lemon** juice
8 thin slices of **light rye**
   or **whole-wheat bread**
**sea salt** and **black pepper**

Place the garlic heads in a roasting pan and drizzle with half the olive oil. Place in a preheated oven, at 375°F, for 45 minutes–1 hour, or until the cloves are soft.

About 15 minutes before the end of cooking time, brush the bread with the remaining olive oil, arrange on a baking sheet, and place in the oven with the garlic until golden and crisp.

Remove the garlic from the oven and cut the heads in half horizontally. Squeeze or scoop out the soft pulp into a bowl. Add any olive oil from the pan, season to taste, and stir in the lemon juice. Mash to a smooth puree and spread on the crostini. Serve hot or cold.

# SESAME SNAPS

While these little snaps are high in sugar, the sesame seeds make them highly nutritious—but stick to one or two!

**Preparation time:** 5 minutes, plus cooling
**Cooking time:** 10 minutes
**Makes 24**
..................

1⅓ cups **sesame seeds**, toasted
⅓ cup firmly packed **brown sugar**
1 cup **wild honey**

Place all the ingredients in a heavy saucepan over medium heat and bring to a boil. Reduce the heat and cook gently, stirring frequently, for 8–10 minutes, or until the mixture becomes thick, syrupy and a slightly darker brown.
.........................................

Pour the mixture on a baking sheet lined with nonstick parchment paper, spread out evenly with a spatula, and smooth the surface. Let cool for a few minutes, then cut into pieces. Let cool completely before serving.
.................................................................

The sesame snaps can be stored in an airtight container for up to 2 weeks.
.................................................................

# SMOKED SALMON & AVOCADO CORNETS

Salmon and avocado boost happiness, while nori promotes the health of the thyroid, which governs energy levels.

**Preparation time:** 25 minutes,
   plus draining, standing and cooling
**Cooking time:** 15 minutes
**Serves 4**

1 cup **glutinous rice** or **risotto rice**
1 cup **water**
⅓ cup **Japanese rice vinegar**
2 tablespoons **sugar**
½ teaspoon **salt**
6 sheets of **sushi nori seaweed**, quartered
8 oz **smoked salmon**, cut into strips
1 **avocado**, peeled, pitted, sliced,
   and drizzled with lemon juice
½ teaspoon **wasabi paste**
1 tablespoon **Japanese pickled ginger**
handful of baby **watercress** leaves
**shoyu** (Japanese soy sauce), to serve

Place the rice in a large bowl, cover with cold water, and stir it, using your fingers. Drain and repeat 2 or 3 times until the water becomes clear. Let drain in a fine strainer for at least 30 minutes.

Place the rice and measured water in a heavy saucepan over medium heat and bring to a boil. Reduce the heat, cover, and cook for 12 minutes, until tender. Remove the pan from the heat and stand, covered, for 15 minutes.

Mix the rice vinegar, sugar, and salt in a bowl. Spread the rice on a flat plate, sprinkle with the vinegar mixture, and stir it in. Cover with a damp cloth and let cool.

Make the cornets by spreading a little of the rice on each of the squares of sushi nori and arranging a piece of salmon and a slice of avocado on top. Add a smear of wasabi and a little ginger and watercress, then roll into cornets, wetting the edge of the nori with a little water to make it stick. Serve with a bowl of shoyu for dipping.

# FIG & APRICOT OAT BARS

These chewy oat bars are packed with nutrients and plenty of slow-release carbohydrates to ward off hunger.

**Preparation time:** 10 minutes
**Cooking time:** 30 minutes
**Makes 12**

1½ sticks **butter**
½ cup **superfine** or **granulated sugar**
¾ cup **maple syrup**
2¼ cups **rolled oats**
⅓ cup chopped soft **dried apricots**
¼ cup **ground almonds**
¼ cup chopped **almonds**
⅔ cup **golden raisins** or **raisins**
2 teaspoons **sesame seeds**
1 teaspoon **ground cinnamon**
6 ripe **figs**, thinly sliced

Put 1¼ sticks of the butter, the sugar, and the maple syrup in a large saucepan over medium heat and cook until the butter has melted and the mixture begins to bubble.

Stir in the oats, apricots, almonds, golden raisins, sesame seeds, and cinnamon and stir to combine.

Transfer the mixture to a greased baking sheet and press down to make an even layer at least ½ inch thick. Sprinkle the figs over the top and dot with the remaining butter.

Place in a preheated oven, at 350°F, for 25 minutes, or until lightly golden. Let cool on the baking sheet, then cut into 12 squares. Store in an airtight container for up to a week.

# STRAWBERRY & BANANA MUFFINS

These moist muffins contain whole-wheat flour to stabilize blood sugar and are perfect for a snack or for breakfast.

**Preparation time:** 10 minutes
**Cooking time:** 20 minutes
**Makes 12**
................

2 **eggs**, lightly beaten
⅓ cup plus 1 tablespoon **applesauce**
¼ cup **canola oil**
¾ cup firmly packed **dark brown sugar**
2 teaspoons **vanilla extract**
2 teaspoons **ground cinnamon**,
   plus extra for dusting
¼ teaspoon **sea salt**
3 very ripe **bananas**, mashed
2 cups **whole-wheat flour**
1 teaspoon **baking soda**
½ teaspoon **baking powder**
1½ cups sliced fresh or frozen
   **strawberries**

Put the eggs into a large bowl with the applesauce, canola oil, sugar, vanilla, cinnamon, salt, and bananas and stir until well combined.

........................................

Mix the flour with the baking soda and baking powder in a separate bowl, then add to the banana mixture and stir to just combine, being careful to avoid overmixing or the muffins will be tough. Lightly fold in the strawberries.

........................................................

Spoon the batter into a 12-section muffin pan lined with paper liners and sprinkle each muffin with a little cinnamon.

........................................................

Place in a preheated oven, at 375°F, for 20 minutes, or until the muffins are golden and risen. Remove from the pan and let cool on a wire rack. The muffins can be stored in an airtight container for up to 4 days.

........................................................

# BLUEBERRY & MINT SMOOTHIE

Smoothies are quick and easy snacks and also make a nourishing breakfast when you are in a rush.

**Preparation time:** 10 minutes
**Serves 4**
................

large bunch of **mint**
2½ cups frozen **blueberries**
2½ cups **soy milk**

Remove the leaves from the bunch of mint and reserve a few for decoration. Put the remaining leaves with the blueberries and soy milk into a blender or food processor and blend until smooth.
..............................................

Pour the mixture into 4 tall glasses, decorate with the reserved mint leaves, and serve immediately.
..............................................

# BANANA & SUNFLOWER SEED COOKIES

You could exchange half the sunflower seeds in these mood-lifting cookies for the same weight of dark chocolate.

**Preparation time:** 10 minutes, plus chilling
**Cooking time:** 15 minutes
**Makes 36**

1²⁄₃ cups **all-purpose flour**
1 teaspoon **baking soda**
2 very ripe **bananas**, mashed
1 stick **butter**, softened
½ cup firmly packed **light brown sugar**
1 teaspoon **vanilla extract**
¾ cup **sunflower seeds**

Put the flour and baking soda into a bowl, mix to combine, then set aside. Put the bananas, butter, sugar, and vanilla into a large bowl and beat until fluffy and combined.

Fold in the flour mixture, a little at a time, until well mixed, then stir in the sunflower seeds. Cover the bowl with plastic wrap and chill in the refrigerator for 1 hour.

Place tablespoons of the cookie dough, well spaced, on 2 baking sheets lined with nonstick parchment paper. Place in a preheated oven, at 350°F, for about 12 minutes, or until lightly golden. Let cool a little on the baking sheets, then transfer to a wire rack to cool completely. The cookies can be stored in an airtight container for up to a week.

# OLIVE & SUN-DRIED TOMATO BISCUITS

Because these biscuits are made with whole-wheat flour, you won't experience an energy dip after eating them.

**Preparation time:** 15 minutes, plus cooling
**Cooking time:** 12 minutes
**Makes 8**

2 cups **whole-wheat flour**, plus extra
    for dusting
1 teaspoon **baking powder**
1 teaspoon **baking soda**
6 tablespoons **butter**, cubed
¼ cup pitted **olives**, chopped
8 **sun-dried tomatoes**, chopped
1 tablespoon chopped **parsley**
1 extra-large **egg**, beaten
¼ cup **buttermilk**, plus extra for brushing

Put the flour, baking powder, baking soda, and butter into a blender or food processor and pulse until the mixture resembles fine bread crumbs. Alternatively, rub the butter into the flour with your fingertips.

Stir in the olives, tomatoes, and parsley, then add the egg and buttermilk and stir with a blunt knife until the mixture comes together.

Transfer the dough to a lightly floured surface and gently press it down to a thickness of 1 inch. Use a 2 inch cookie cutter to cut out the biscuits, rerolling the scraps as necessary.

Arrange on a lightly floured baking sheet, brush with a little buttermilk, and place in a preheated oven, at 425°F, for about 12 minutes, until golden and risen. Transfer to a wire rack to cool.

# LENTIL & PEA SOUP

Lentils are versatile whole grains with a host of health benefits. Here, they are combined with peas and fragrant herbs.

**Preparation time:** 15 minutes
**Cooking time:** 25 minutes
**Serves 4**

1 teaspoon **olive oil**
1 **leek**, finely sliced
1 **garlic clove**, crushed
2 cups rinsed, drained canned or cooked **green lentils**
3¾ cups **vegetable stock**
2 tablespoons chopped **mixed herbs**, such as thyme, oregano, tarragon, mint, and parsley
1⅓ cups **frozen peas**
2 tablespoons **crème fraîche** or **sour cream**
2 tablespoons chopped **fresh mint**
**sea salt** and **black pepper**

Heat the oil in a large saucepan over medium heat, add the leek and garlic, and cook for 5–6 minutes, until softened.

Add the lentils, stock, and herbs, bring to a boil, reduce the heat, and simmer, covered, for 10 minutes. Add the peas and continue to cook for 5 minutes.

Remove from the heat, let cool a little, then transfer half the soup to a blender or food processor and blend until smooth. Return to the pan, stir to combine with the unblended soup, then heat through and season to taste.

Stir together the crème fraîche and mint. Ladle the soup into warm bowls and serve immediately with the crème fraîche on the side.

# MINTED KALE SOUP

This warm, buttery soup is filling and positively bursting with nutrients to nourish, soothe, and heal.

**Preparation time:** 15 minutes
**Cooking time:** 30 minutes
**Serves 4**

.................

2 tablespoons **butter**
2 tablespoons **olive oil**
1 large **onion**, chopped
2 **garlic cloves**, chopped
3 **potatoes**, peeled and chopped
2 cups rinsed, drained canned **lima beans**
4 cups **chicken**
   or **vegetable stock**
4½ cups shredded **kale**
   (remove the thick stems)
¼ cup chopped **mint**, plus
   a few whole leaves to garnish
**sea salt** and **black pepper**

**To serve**
**rye toast** or **spelt bread**, to serve
⅓ cup **plain yogurt with live active cultures**
   or **crème fraîche** (optional)

Heat the butter and oil in a large saucepan over medium heat and add the onion. Cook for about 5 minutes, until starting to soften, then add the garlic and potatoes.

..................................................

Stir in the beans and stock, bring to a boil, reduce the heat, and simmer for about 15 minutes, stirring and skimming frequently. Add the kale and mint and continue cooking for another 5 minutes, until the vegetables are tender.

..................................................

Remove from the heat, cool slightly, then transfer to a blender or food processor and blend until smooth. Season to taste and ladle the soup into warm bowls. Garnish with mint leaves and serve with rye toast or spelt bread, and a swirl of yogurt, if desired.

..................................................

# TURKEY SOUP WITH LEMON & BARLEY

This warming soup is surprisingly light and full of nutrient-rich, energy-boosting barley and calming turkey.

**Preparation time:** 15 minutes
**Cooking time:** 40 minutes
**Serves 4**

2 tablespoons **olive oil**
1 large **onion**, finely chopped
3 **garlic cloves**, finely chopped
1 teaspoon **ground turmeric**
½ teaspoon **ground cinnamon**
½ teaspoon **ground cumin**
½ teaspoon **ground cardamom**
½ inch piece of fresh **ginger root**,
    peeled and finely chopped
finely grated zest and juice of 2 **lemons**
5 cups **chicken** or **vegetable stock**
¾ cup **pearl barley**
2 cups shredded **cooked turkey**
2 cups chopped fresh **cilantro**,
    plus extra to garnish
**sea salt** and **black pepper**

Heat the oil in a large saucepan over medium-low heat, add the onion, and cook gently until softened and just beginning to brown. Stir in the garlic and cook for another minute, then add the turmeric, cinnamon, cumin, cardamom, and ginger.

Add the lemon zest, lemon juice, and stock and bring to a boil. Reduce the heat to a slow simmer and add the barley. Cover and cook for about 25 minutes, stirring occasionally, until the barley is tender but still has a little bite.

Add the turkey and cilantro and season to taste. Cook, uncovered, for another 5 minutes, then ladle the soup into warm bowls and garnish with chopped cilantro.

# BROCCOLI & ALMOND SOUP

This light soup provides brain-supporting omega oils as well as protection from the harmful side effects of stress.

**Preparation time:** 15 minutes
**Cooking time:** 20 minutes
**Serves 4**

2 tablespoons **butter**
1 **onion**, coarsely chopped
1 head of **broccoli**, coarsely chopped
⅓ cup **ground almonds**
3¾ cups **vegetable** or **chicken stock**
2 teaspoons **dried thyme**
1¼ cups **milk**
**sea salt** and **black pepper**

**To serve**
1 tablespoon **butter**
¼ cup **almonds**, crushed
⅓ cup **plain yogurt with live active cultures**

Heat the butter in a large saucepan over medium heat, add the onion, and cook gently for 5 minutes, until just beginning to soften. Stir in the broccoli until coated in the butter, then add the ground almonds, stock, and thyme and season to taste.

Bring to a boil, reduce the heat, and simmer, covered, for 10 minutes, until the broccoli is just tender and still bright green.

Meanwhile, for the garnish, heat the butter in a skillet, add the almonds, and sauté for a few minutes, stirring constantly, until golden.

Remove the soup from the heat, let cool a little, then transfer in batches to a blender or food processor and blend until finely speckled with green. Pour the soup back into the saucepan and stir in the milk. Reheat and season to taste.

Ladle the soup into warm bowls, drizzle with the yogurt, and sprinkle with the almonds. Serve immediately.

# MISO BROTH WITH SHRIMP

With shrimp to boost immunity, libido, and virility, this easy recipe will become a lunchtime standby on busy days.

**Preparation time:** 10 minutes
**Cooking time:** 10 minutes
**Serves 6**

4 **scallions** or **baby leeks**, thinly sliced
¾ inch piece of fresh **ginger root**, finely chopped
½–1 large **red chile**, seeded and thinly sliced
6⅓ cups **fish** or **vegetable stock**
3 tablespoons **miso paste**
2 tablespoons **mirin** (Japanese cooking wine)
1 tablespoon **dark soy sauce**
1½ cups thinly sliced **bok choy**
2 tablespoons chopped fresh **cilantro**
5 oz cooked peeled **shrimp**
1 small **avocado**, peeled, pitted, and chopped

Place the white parts of the scallions or leeks into a saucepan with the ginger, chile, stock, miso, mirin, and soy sauce. Bring to a boil, reduce the heat, and simmer for 5 minutes.

Stir in the green parts of the scallions or leeks, the bok choy, cilantro, and shrimp and cook for 2–3 minutes or until the bok choy has just wilted. Ladle the soup into warm bowls and sprinkle with the chopped avocado. Serve immediately.

# GOAT CHEESE, APPLE & BROCCOLI SALAD

With a host of mood-lifting nutrients, this salad is ideal as a warming lunch or an appetizer for a special dinner.

**Preparation time:** 20 minutes
**Cooking time:** 5 minutes
**Serves 4**
................

1 tablespoon **olive oil**, plus extra for brushing
1 tablespoon **lemon juice**
1 teaspoon **dried thyme**
3½ cups **mixed salad greens**
1 head of **broccoli**, cut into small florets
2 **Granny Smith apples**, peeled, cored, and thinly sliced
2 **goat cheese** logs, cut into ½ inch slices
¼ cup **Manuka honey**
**sea salt** and **black pepper**

Mix the olive oil, lemon juice, and thyme in a small bowl and season to taste. Arrange the salad greens, broccoli, and half the apple slices on a large plate, drizzle with the dressing, and toss until coated.
................

Place the goat cheese on a lightly greased baking sheet and brush with a little olive oil. Place in a preheated oven, at 400°F, for about 5 minutes or until starting to brown.
................

Meanwhile, place the honey and remaining apple in a food processor or blender and blend until smooth. Transfer to a small saucepan and heat for 2–3 minutes, until just warm.
................

Arrange the warm cheese on the salad and drizzle with the honey mixture. Sprinkle with black pepper and serve immediately.
................

# FIG, RASPBERRY & PROSCIUTTO SALAD

Sweet and salty, this fresh salad is quick to make, and it provides a boost of fiber, antioxidants, and protein.

**Preparation time:** 5 minutes
**Serves 4**

5 cups **arugula and beet leaf salad**
6 ripe **figs**, halved
1 cup **raspberries**
8 slices of **prosciutto**
2 tablespoons aged **balsamic vinegar**
2 tablespoons **olive oil**
10 oz **mozzarella**

Arrange the salad greens on a large serving plate with the figs, raspberries, and prosciutto. Whisk together the vinegar and oil to make a dressing.

Tear the mozzarella into large pieces and arrange on top of the salad. Drizzle the dressing on top and serve immediately.

# RARE BEEF & BABY BEET SALAD

Combined with iron-rich beef, horseradish is a natural digestive and adds piquancy to this mood-enhancing salad.

**Preparation time:** 20 minutes
**Cooking time:** 25 minutes
**Serves 4**

8 oz unpeeled **baby beets**,
    stems removed
1 lb **top sirloin** or **tenderloin steak**,
    trimmed
2 teaspoons **olive oil**
finely grated zest of 1 **lemon**
1 **garlic clove**, finely chopped
2 tablespoons finely snipped **chives**
2 cups sliced **green beans**
10 **radishes**, thinly sliced
½ cup **walnut** pieces
4 cups **mixed salad greens**
1½ tablespoons **lemon juice**
1 teaspoon **horseradish sauce**
1 teaspoon **honey**
3 tablespoons **reduced-fat sour cream**
**sea salt** and **black pepper**

Cook the beets in a saucepan of lightly salted boiling water for 15–25 minutes, depending on their size, until tender.

Meanwhile, place the steak in a shallow dish with the olive oil, lemon zest, garlic, half the chives, and plenty of black pepper. Toss until the meat is well coated in the marinade.

Cook the green beans in another saucepan of lightly salted boiling water for 1–2 minutes, until almost tender. Drain and refresh in cold water.

Heat a ridged grill pan over medium-high heat and cook the steak for 1 minute on each side, until charred but still pink inside. Set aside in a warm place to rest.

Drain the beets, cut into wedges, and toss with the beans, radishes, walnuts, and salad greens, then pile onto serving plates.

Mix the lemon juice, horseradish, honey, sour cream, and remaining chives in a bowl and season to taste. Slice the beef thinly and arrange on top of the salads, drizzle with the horseradish dressing, and serve immediately.

# TURKEY & PEANUT NOODLE SALAD

Both peanuts and poultry contain high-quality protein and help to boost levels of feel-good serotonin.

**Preparation time:** 15 minutes
**Cooking time:** 15 minutes
**Serves 4**

12 oz **brown rice noodles**
1½ cups **sugarsnap peas**
8 **baby corn**
1 tablespoon **sesame oil**
1 teaspoon **olive oil**
1¼ lb boneless, skinless
   **turkey**, cubed
3 tablespoons **sweet chili sauce**
1 tablespoon **dark soy sauce**

4 **scallions**, finely sliced
⅔ cup **peanuts**, lightly toasted
2 cups coarsely chopped fresh **cilantro**

**Dressing**
1 tablespoon **olive oil**
1 tablespoon **Thai fish sauce**
1 teaspoon **hot chili sauce**
1 tablespoon **dark soy sauce**
1 **garlic clove**, finely chopped
finely grated zest and juice of 2 limes

Soak the noodles in boiling water until tender, or prepare according to package directions, and drain thoroughly. Meanwhile, cook the sugarsnap peas and baby corn in a saucepan of lightly salted boiling water for 2–3 minutes, then drain and refresh in cold water.

Heat a large skillet or wok over medium heat and add the oils, followed by the turkey. Cook, stirring often, until golden. Add the sweet chili sauce and soy sauce and continue cooking for 4–5 minutes, or until the turkey is cooked through.

Place all the dressing ingredients in a screw-top jar and shake vigorously until well combined. Arrange the noodles, sugarsnap peas, and corn in a large bowl, drizzle with the dressing, and toss to coat.

Place the scallions, peanuts, cilantro, and turkey on top and toss lightly again. Serve warm or at room temperature.

# BEET, GRAPE & FETA SALAD

With tangy grapes, salty feta, and sweet beets, this is antioxidant heaven, designed to promote overall well-being.

**Preparation time:** 20 minutes
**Cooking time:** 25 minutes
**Serves 4**

8 large **beets**, peeled
    and cut into chunks
2 tablespoons **olive oil**
1 cup **grapes**, halved
4 cups **mixed salad greens**
4 **scallions**, finely sliced
2 tablespoons **walnut oil**
2 tablespoons **balsamic vinegar**
1 teaspoon **dried thyme**
1 cup crumbled **feta cheese**
⅓ cup **pine nuts**, lightly toasted
**sea salt** and **black pepper**

Place the beet chunks on a nonstick baking sheet, drizzle with the olive oil, and season to taste. Use your hands to toss the beets in the oil until evenly coated.

Place in a preheated oven, at 400°F, for about 25 minutes, turning once or twice. About 10 minutes before the end of cooking, add half the grapes and cook until just starting to brown.

Arrange the salad greens on 4 serving plates and sprinkle with the scallions. Mix the walnut oil, balsamic vinegar, and thyme in a small bowl and season to taste.

Remove the beets and grapes from the oven and let cool slightly. Arrange on the salad greens, sprinkle with the remaining grapes, the feta, and pine nuts, and lightly toss. Drizzle with the balsamic dressing and serve immediately.

# SALAD NIÇOISE WITH ARTICHOKES & ASPARAGUS

This satisfying salad contains enough protein to keep blood sugar levels stable and appetites fully sated.

**Preparation time:** 15 minutes
**Cooking time:** 2 minutes
**Serves 4**

12–16 **asparagus** spears, trimmed
1 large **romaine lettuce**, coarsely shredded
4 hard-boiled **eggs**, shelled and quartered
12 **artichoke hearts** from a jar, halved
1 (5 oz) can **tuna** in water,
    drained and flaked
16 **black olives**, pitted
16 **cherry tomatoes**, halved
1 large **avocado**, peeled,
    pitted, and chopped
**crusty whole-wheat bread**, to serve

**Dressing**
¼ cup **red wine vinegar**
1 teaspoon **Dijon mustard**
½ cup **olive oil**
2 **garlic cloves**, crushed
1 teaspoon **dried thyme**
1 teaspoon **wild honey**
**sea salt** and **black pepper**

Cook the asparagus in a steamer over a saucepan of gently simmering water for 2 minutes, then refresh in cold water. Place all the dressing ingredients in a screw-top jar and shake vigorously until well combined.

Arrange the lettuce in a large bowl or serving plate and place the eggs, artichokes, tuna, olives, tomatoes, avocado, parsley, and asparagus on top.

Drizzle with the dressing and toss lightly until well coated. Serve with warm, crusty whole-wheat bread.

# TOMATO, TOFU & HOT PEPPER SALAD

The soy in the tofu is an excellent hormone balancer, while hot peppers are both warming and good for the digestion.

**Preparation time:** 10 minutes
**Serves 4**

4 **beefsteak tomatoes**, thinly sliced
8 oz **tofu**, crumbled
½ cup drained and thinly sliced **hot piquanté peppers** from a jar
⅓ cup snipped **chives**
¼ cup chopped **flat leaf parsley**
⅓ cup **pine nuts**, toasted
½ cup **golden raisins**
½ cup **olive oil**
½ cup **lemon juice**
4 teaspoons **sugar**
**sea salt** and **black pepper**
**whole-wheat bread**, to serve

Arrange the tomato slices on 4 serving plates, lightly seasoning the layers to taste. Put the tofu into a mixing bowl with the piquanté peppers, chives, parsley, pine nuts, and golden raisins and toss together.

Whisk the olive oil with the lemon juice and sugar in a small bowl, season lightly and stir into the tofu mixture. Spoon the tofu mixture over the tomatoes and serve with whole-wheat bread.

# WARM RAINBOW SALAD

Delicious, fragrant, and teeming with nutrients, this beautiful warm salad is packed with loads of different vegetables.

**Preparation time:** 20 minutes
**Cooking time:** 20–25 minutes
**Serves 4**

10 oz **baby new potatoes**
1 **red bell pepper**, cored, seeded, and sliced
1 **yellow bell pepper**, cored, seeded, and sliced
1 tablespoon **olive oil**
1 tablespoon chopped **thyme**
1 large **beet**, peeled and coarsely grated
1 large **carrot**, coarsely grated
1 large **avocado**, peeled, pitted, and chopped
5 cups colorful **mixed salad greens**
¼ cup crushed **walnuts**
**sea salt** and **black pepper**

**Dressing**
2 tablespoons **walnut oil**
1 tablespoon **shallot vinegar**
1 tablespoon **Dijon mustard**
pinch of **sugar**

Place the potatoes and bell peppers in a large roasting pan, drizzle with the olive oil and thyme, and season to taste. Toss to coat the vegetables in the oil, then place in a preheated oven, at 375°F, for 20–25 minutes, until tender.

Meanwhile, toss the beet, carrot, and avocado with the salad greens and divide among 4 serving plates. Place all the dressing ingredients in a screw-top jar, season to taste, and shake vigorously to combine.

Arrange the warm vegetables on the plates on top of the salads and drizzle with the dressing. Sprinkle with the walnuts and serve immediately.

# GINGER SCALLOPS WITH ASPARAGUS

Scallops not only boost virility, libido, and immunity, but provide energy and balance blood sugar levels.

**Preparation time:** 10 minutes,
   plus marinating
**Cooking time:** 10 minutes
**Serves 4**
................

12 large **scallops**
2 **scallions**, thinly sliced
finely grated zest of 1 **lime**
1 tablespoon **ginger syrup**
2 tablespoons **olive oil**, plus
   extra for drizzling
8 oz fine **asparagus** spears
4 oz **sea asparagus**
2 tablespoons **lime juice**
2 large handfuls of **mixed salad greens**
handful of **chervil**
**sea salt** and **black pepper**

Rinse the scallops and pat dry. Cut in half horizontally and place in a bowl with the scallions, lime zest, ginger syrup, and half the oil. Season to taste, toss well, and set aside to marinate for 15 minutes.

..........................................................

Meanwhile, cook the asparagus in a steamer over a saucepan of gently simmering water for 5–8 minutes, adding the sea asparagus for the last 2–3 minutes. Toss with the remaining oil and the lime juice, season to taste, and keep warm.

..........................................................

Heat a large, nonstick skillet until hot, add the scallops, and cook for 1 minute on each side, until golden and just cooked through. Add the marinade juices to the skillet and remove from the heat.

..........................................................

Arrange the asparagus, sea asparagus, salad greens, and chervil on 4 serving plates, top with the scallops and pan juices, and serve immediately.

..........................................................

# MACKEREL & ASPARAGUS TART

Mackerel and asparagus are nutrient-rich functional foods that lift mood and encourage healthy brain function.

---

**Preparation time:** 20 minutes, plus chilling
**Cooking time:** 30–40 minutes
**Serves 4**

................

8 **asparagus** spears, trimmed
8 oz **smoked mackerel**,
   skin and bones removed
2 **eggs**
½ cup **milk**
2 tablespoons finely chopped **dill**
½ cup **heavy cream**
**sea salt** and **black pepper**

**Pastry dough**
1⅔ cups **all-purpose flour**,
   plus extra for dusting
6 tablespoons **butter**, chilled and diced
1 **egg**, plus 1 **egg yolk**

**To serve**
2 **avocados**, peeled, pitted, and sliced
2 tablespoons **lemon juice**

Knead the dough lightly for 1 minute, until smooth, wrap in plasti wrap, and chill in the refrigerator for at least 30 minutes.

...................................................................

Roll out the dough on a well-floured surface until it is about ⅛ inch thick and use to line a 10 inch round tart pan. Chill the pastry shell for 1 hour.

...........................

Line the pastry shell with nonstick parchmnent paper, fill with dried beans or rice, then place in a preheated oven, at 350°F, for 10–12 minutes, until lightly golden. Remove the parchment paper and beans and cook for another 2 minutes.

...................................................................

Meanwhile, steam the asparagus for 3–4 minutes, then refresh in cold water. Cut each spear into 3 pieces.

...............................................

Flake the fish into the pastry shell and add the asparagus. Beat together the eggs, milk, dill, and cream and season to taste. Pour the mixture into the pastry shell and return to the oven for 20–25 minutes, until just set. Toss the avocado slices with the lemon juice and serve with the tart.

...................................................................

# SESAME-CRUSTED SALMON

Sesame seeds have a powerful antidepressant effect and provide the basis for this healthy, restorative dinner.

**Preparation time:** 10 minutes
**Cooking time:** 12–15 minutes
**Serves 4**

¼ cup **sesame seeds**
1 teaspoon dried **red pepper flakes**
4 **salmon fillets**, about 4 oz each
2 teaspoons **olive oil**
2 **carrots**, cut into matchsticks
2 **red bell peppers**, cored, seeded, and thinly sliced
8 oz **shiitake mushrooms**, halved
2 **bok choy**, quartered lengthwise
4 **scallions**, shredded
1 tablespoon **dark soy sauce**
**basmati** or **long-grain rice**, to serve

Mix the sesame seeds and red pepper flakes on a plate, then press the salmon fillets into the mixture to coat.

Heat half the oil in a nonstick skillet over medium heat, add the salmon, and cook for 3–4 minutes on each side, until cooked through. Remove from the skillet and keep warm.

Heat the remaining oil in the skillet over high heat, add the vegetables, and stir-fry for 3–4 minutes, until just cooked. Drizzle the soy sauce over the vegetables and serve with the salmon and basmati rice.

# MACKEREL FILLETS WITH OAT TOPPING

Rich in healthy omega-3 oils, fresh mackerel fillets with
a crunchy oat crust make a quick and delicious meal.

**Preparation time:** 15 minutes
**Cooking time:** 5 minutes
**Serves 4**

4 large **mackerel fillets**, boned
2 teaspoons **Dijon mustard**
2 teaspoons **horseradish sauce**
finely grated zest of ½ **lemon**
½ teaspoon **sea salt**
½ teaspoon **black pepper**
⅓ cup **rolled oats**
2 tablespoons **butter**

**To serve**
**watercress**
steamed **broccoli**
**lemon** wedges

Place the mackerel fillets on a board, skin
side down, and pat dry with paper towels.
Mix the mustard, horseradish, lemon
zest, salt, and black pepper in a small
bowl and spread evenly over the tops
of the fillets. Press the oats firmly onto
the mustard mixture.

Heat the butter in a large skillet over
medium heat. When it begins to foam,
put the mackerel fillets inot the skillet,
oat side down, and cook for 2–3 minutes.

Carefully turn over the mackerel and
cook for another 1–2 minutes, until
cooked through. Serve the fish fillets
on a bed of watercress, with broccoli
and lemon wedges on the side.

# STIR-FRIED TOFU WITH SHRIMP & RICE NOODLES

With zinc-rich shrimp, brown rice noodles, and mood-lifting soybeans in the tofu, this dish has all you need to get happy.

**Preparation time:** 10 minutes, plus standing
**Cooking time:** 10 minutes
**Serves 4**

1 lb **tofu**
⅓ cup **dark soy sauce**
2 tablespoons **honey**
2 tablespoons **peanut oil**
6 cups shredded **collard greens**
1¼ lb precooked **brown rice noodles**
(or 8 oz uncooked brown rice
noodles, prepared according to
package directions)
1 lb cooked peeled **shrimp**
½ cup **hoisin sauce**
2 cups fresh **cilantro**, chopped

Pat the tofu dry with paper towles and cut into ¾ inch dice. Mix the soy sauce and honey together in a bowl, add the tofu, and mix gently. Let stand for 5 minutes.

Drain the tofu, reserving the marinade, and pat the cubes dry with paper towels. Heat the oil in a large skillet over high heat and cook the tofu for 5 minutes, stirring frequently, until it is crisp and golden. Remove from the skillet and keep warm.

Add the greens to the skillet and cook quickly, stirring, until wilted. Return the tofu to the skillet with the noodles and shrimp and toss together the ingredients for 2 minutes, until heated through.

Mix the hoisin sauce with the reserved marinade. Drizzle the liquid over the stir-fry, mix well, sprinkle with the cilantro, and serve immediately.

# RED SNAPPER WITH CAPERS & WARM TOMATO SALAD

Red snapper is a light fish, rich in nutrients, which complements this stress-busting tomato salad.

**Preparation time:** 20 minutes
**Cooking time:** 10 minutes
**Serves 4**

8 small **red snapper fillets**
finely grated zest of 1 **lemon**
2 teaspoons baby **capers**, rinsed and
    drained
2 **scallions**, finely sliced
2½ cups mixed **red** and **yellow**
    **cherry tomatoes**
1½ cups trimmed fine **green beans**
2 **garlic cloves**, finely chopped
1 (2 oz) can **anchovy fillets**,
    drained and chopped
1 tablespoon **olive oil**
2 tablespoons **lemon juice**
2 tablespoons chopped **parsley**
**sea salt** and **black pepper**
**caper berries**, to garnish
**sourdough bread**, to serve

Tear off 4 large sheets of aluminum foil and line with nonstick parchment paper. Put 2 red snapper fillets on each piece of parchment paper, then sprinkle with the lemon zest, capers, and scallions and season to taste. Fold over the paper-lined foil and scrunch together the edges to seal. Place the packages on a large baking sheet.

Put the cherry tomatoes in an ovenproof dish with the green beans, garlic, anchovies, oil, and lemon juice. Season to taste and mix well. Place in a preheated oven, at 400°F, for about 10 minutes, until tender. Place the fish in the oven at the same time, for 8–10 minutes, until the flesh flakes easily when pressed with a knife.

Spoon the vegetables onto warm serving plates and top with the fish. Sprinkle with the chopped parsley, garnish with cape berries, and serve immediately with sourdough bread.

# CHICKEN & PEANUT STEW WITH BROWN RICE

This is a traditional Ghanaian dish with a few alterations. It's easy to make and older children love it, too.

**Preparation time:** 10 minutes
**Cooking time:** 30–35 minutes
**Serves 4**

1 **onion**, coarsely chopped
3 **garlic cloves**, unpeeled, coarsely chopped
2 inch piece of fresh **ginger root**, peeled and coarsely chopped
1 **red chile**, seeded and coarsely chopped
2 tablespoons **olive oil**
8 boneless, skinless **chicken thighs**, cut into bite-size pieces
1 (14½ oz) can **diced tomatoes**
2½ cups **chicken** or **vegetable stock**
¼ cup **peanut butter**
**sea salt** and **black pepper**
3 tablespoons roasted **peanuts**, to garnish
**brown rice**, to serve

Put the onion, garlic, ginger, and chile into a blender or food processor and blend until smooth. Heat the oil in a large saucepan over medium heat, add the onion mixture, and cook for 2–3 minutes, until fragrant.

Add the chicken and cook for 2–3 minutes, turning frequently, until browned all over. Stir in the tomatoes and stock and simmer, uncovered, for 15–20 minutes, until the chicken is cooked through.

Stir in the peanut butter and cook for another 5 minutes. Season to taste and ladle the stew over the brown rice. Serve immediately, garnished with a sprinkling of roasted peanuts.

# CAULIFLOWER & TURKEY BIRYANI

This one-dish dish combines relaxation-inducing turkey with vitamin C-rich cauliflower.

**Preparation time:** 20 minutes
**Cooking time:** 35 minutes
**Serves 4**

12 oz boneless, skinless **turkey** breast, cubed
1 small **cauliflower**, cut into small florets
1 **onion**, thinly sliced
¼ cup **peanut oil**
2 **bay leaves**
3 **cardamom pods**, crushed
1½ cup **basmati** or **other long-grain rice**
3 cups **chicken stock**
1 tablespoon **nigella seeds**
**sea salt** and **black pepper**

**Marinade**
1 **onion**, coarsely chopped
2 **garlic cloves**, chopped
¾ inch piece of fresh **ginger root**, peeled and coarsely chopped
2 teaspoons **ground turmeric**
¼ teaspoon **ground cloves**
½ teaspoon **dried red pepper flakes**
¼ teaspoon **ground cinnamon**
2 teaspoons **medium curry paste**
1 tablespoon **lemon juice**
2 teaspoons **sugar**

**To garnish**
1 **onion**, thinly sliced
2 tablespoons **slivered almonds**, toasted

Put all the marinade ingredients into a blender or food processor and blend until smooth. Transfer to a large bowl, add the turkey, season to taste, mix well, and set aside.

For the garnish, heat 1 tablespoon of the oil in a large skillet over medium heat and cook the onion until golden and crisp. Remove with a slotted spoon, drain on paper towels, and set aside.

Add the cauliflower to the skillet and sauté gently for 5 minutes. Add the remaining onion and cook, stirring, for about 5 minutes, until the cauliflower is softened and golden. Drain on paper towels and set aside.

Heat the remaining oil in the skillet. Add the turkey and marinade and cook gently for 5 minutes, stirring frequently. Add the bay leaves, cardamom, rice, and stock and bring to a boil. Reduce the heat and simmer gently, stirring occasionally, for 10–12 minutes, until the rice is tender and the stock has been absorbed, adding a little water if the mixture becomes too dry.

Stir in the nigella seeds and cauliflower and heat through. Serve immediately, garnished with the crispy onion and almonds.

# TURKEY, LENTIL & APRICOT STEW

This aromatic stew is easy to make and freezes well, so double the quantities for a healthy meal to serve another time.

**Preparation time:** 15 minutes
**Cooking time:** 30 minutes
**Serves 4**
................

2 tablespoons **olive oil**
1 large **onion**, finely chopped
1 inch piece of fresh **ginger root**,
    peeled and grated
2 **garlic cloves**, finely chopped
1 teaspoon **black pepper**
1 teaspoon **ground coriander**
1 teaspoon **ground cinnamon**
1 teaspoon **ground cloves**
1 teaspoon **ground cumin**
½ teaspoon **ground cardamom**
2 teaspoons **paprika**
1 teaspoon grated **nutmeg**
1 lb boneless, skinless **turkey**,
    cut into chunks
¾ cup **red lentils**
2½ cups **vegetable** or **chicken stock**
finely grated zest and juice of 1 **lemon**
⅓ cup diced soft **dried apricots**
2 cups chopped fresh **cilantro**

Heat the oil in a large saucepan over medium heat, add the onion, ginger, and garlic, and cook for about 5 minutes, until the onion is beginning to soften.

.......................................................

Place the spices in a bowl and stir to mix. Add the turkey chunks and stir well to coat evenly. Add to the pan and cook for 5 minutes, stirring frequently, until browned all over.

...............................

Add the lentils and mix gently, then add the stock, lemon zest, lemon juice, apricots, and half the cilantro. Bring to a boil, reduce the heat, and simmer for about 15 minutes, or until the turkey is cooked through and the lentils are tender. Add the remaining cilantro and ladle into big bowls to serve.

.......................................................

# THAI TURKEY BURGERS WITH CRISPY KALE

These flavorsome burgers are ideal for relaxed family meals and offer a good hit of mood-lifting tryptophan.

**Preparation time:** 20 minutes
**Cooking time:** 20 minutes
**Serves 4**
................

1 lb **ground turkey thigh** meat
4 **scallions**, finely chopped
½ inch piece of fresh **ginger root**,
    peeled and grated
1 **garlic clove**, crushed
1 **lemon grass stalk**, outer leaves
    removed and core finely chopped
½ **red chile**, seeded and finely chopped
2 tablespoons finely chopped fresh **cilantro**
1 **egg**, lightly beaten
4 **whole-wheat buns**, warmed
**sea salt** and **black pepper**

**Crispy kale**
4½ cups bite-size **kale** pieces
finely grated zest of 1 **lemon**
1 tablespoon **olive oil**
**sesame seeds**, for sprinkling (optional)

To make the crispy kale, put the kale into a large bowl and toss with the lemon zest, olive oil, and a little sea salt. Arrange in a single layer on 1 or 2 baking sheets.
...............

Place in a preheated oven, at 400°F, for 15–20 minutes, turning halfway through cooking time, until crunchy and crisp. Sprinkle with a little more salt or some sesame seeds, if desired.
...............

Meanwhile, put the turkey into a large bowl with the onions, ginger, garlic, lemon grass, chile, and cilantro. Mix well, then season to taste and stir in the egg.
...............

Use your hands to shape the mixture into 4 large balls, then press them firmly into patty shapes. Place under a preheated hot broiler and cook for 5 minutes on each side, or until golden and cooked through. Serve in warm whole-wheat buns with crispy kale on the side.
...............

# THAI BEEF & MIXED PEPPER STIR-FRY

A fragrant, nourishing meal to banish anxiety, depression, and fatigue and encourage restful sleep.

**Preparation time:** 15 minutes
**Cooking time:** 10 minutes
**Serves 4**
................

1 tablespoon **sesame oil**
1 **garlic clove**, finely chopped
1 lb **lean tenderloin steak**,
    thinly sliced across the grain
1 **lemon grass stalk**, outer leaves
    removed and core finely chopped
1 inch piece of fresh **ginger root**,
    peeled and finely chopped
1 **red bell pepper**, cored, seeded,
    and thickly sliced
1 **green bell pepper**, cored,
    seeded, and thickly sliced
1 **onion**, thickly sliced
1 **red chile**, seeded and finely chopped
finely grated zest and juice of 2 **limes**
handful of fresh **cilantro**, chopped
**sea salt** and **black pepper**
**rice** or **noodles** to serve

Heat the oil in a wok or large skillet over high heat, add the garlic and beef, and stir-fry for 2–3 minutes, until lightly browned.

................

Stir in the lemon grass and ginger and remove the pan from the heat. Remove the beef from the pan and set aside.

................

Add the bell peppers, onion, and chile to the pan and stir-fry for 2–3 minutes, until the onions are just turning golden brown and are slightly softened.

................

Return the beef to the pan, stir in the lime zest, lime juice, and cilantro, and season to taste. Serve with rice or noodles.

................

# HERBED ARTICHOKE CASSEROLE

Don't hesitate to add whatever root vegetables you have on hand to this delicious casserole.

**Preparation time:** 15 minutes
**Cooking time:** 30 minutes
**Serves 4**

2 tablespoons **olive oil**
1 large **onion**, chopped
2 **celery sticks**, chopped
3 **carrots**, chopped
2 **parsnips**, chopped
1 **fennel bulb**, outer leaves removed, chopped
1 **sweet potato**, peeled and chopped
2 tablespoons **dried oregano**
1 tablespoon **dried rosemary**
1 teaspoon **dried thyme**
½ teaspoon **dried marjoram**
½ teaspoon **dried basil**
2½ cups **vegetable stock**
2 cups rinsed, drained canned **lima beans**
2 cups rinsed, drained canned **chickpeas**
½ (14 oz) can or jar **artichoke hearts**, rinsed and drained
**sea salt** and **black pepper**
1 tablespoon chopped **oregano**, to garnish
**couscous** or **bulgur wheat**, to serve

Heat the oil in a large saucepan over medium heat, add the onions, celery, carrots, parsnips, fennel, and sweet potato and cook for about 5 minutes, or until the onions begin to soften.

Stir in the dried herbs and continue to cook for another 5 minutes. Add the stock and bring to a boil, reduce the heat, and simmer for 15 minutes, stirring frequently, until the vegetables are tender.

Add the lima beans, chickpeas, and artichokes and continue to simmer for another 5 minutes. Season to taste and serve immediately with couscous or bulgur wheat, garnished with chopped oregano.

# PENNE WITH TOMATO, ARTICHOKE & OLIVE SAUCE

Whole-wheat penne is combined with antioxidant-rich tomatoes, nourishing olives, and hormone-balancing artichokes.

**Preparation time:** 15 minutes
**Cooking time:** 25 minutes
**Serves 4**

................

1 tablespoon **olive oil**
1 **onion**, finely chopped
2 **garlic cloves**, finely chopped
¼ cup **red wine**
1 (28 oz) can **diced tomatoes**
pinch of **sugar**
finely grated zest of ½ **lemon**
1 teaspoon **dried oregano**
¾ cup pitted **black ripe olives**,
    coarsely chopped
1 lb **whole-wheat penne**
small bunch of **basil**, torn
1 (14 oz) can or jar **artichoke hearts**,
rinsed, drained, and chopped
**sea salt** and **black pepper**
**green salad**, to serve

Heat the olive oil in a large, heavy saucepan over medium-low heat, add the onion and garlic, and cook gently for 5–6 minutes, until softened.

..........................

Stir in the wine, tomatoes, sugar, lemon zest, oregano, and olives and bring to a boil. Reduce the heat and simmer gently for 12–15 minutes.

..................................

Meanwhile, cook the pasta in a large saucepan of lightly salted boiling water for 11 minutes, or according to the package directions, until "al dente".

...............................................

Add the basil and artichokes to the pasta sauce and cook gently until heated through. Season to taste, toss with the pasta, and serve with a green salad.

...............................................

# CREAMY ROASTED PEPPERS WITH MIXED GRAINS

Any grains work well in this dinner-time dish, designed to banish anxiety and set you up for a good night's sleep.

**Preparation time:** 10 minutes
**Cooking time:** 25–30 minutes
**Serves 4**

.................

4 long **red sweet peppers**, halved
    lengthwise and seeded
¼ cup **walnut** pieces, chopped
3 cups cooked **mixed grains**,
    such as bulgur wheat, quinoa,
    brown rice, or spelt
2 tablespoons **lemon juice**
2 tablespoons **tomato paste**
3 tablespoons chopped **mixed herbs**,
    such as parsley, tarragon, chives,
    and thyme
**sea salt** and **black pepper**

**Cheese filling**
1½ cups **cream cheese**
3 tablespoons chopped **mixed herbs**,
    such as parsley, tarragon, chives,
    and thyme
finely grated zest of ½ **lemon**
2 tablespoons toasted **mixed seeds**

Mix together all the filling ingredients in a small bowl and season to taste. Arrange the sweet peppers, cut side up, on a baking sheet and spoon in the filling. Sprinkle with the walnuts and place in a preheated oven, at 400°F, for 25–30 minutes, until the peppers are tender and the filling is golden.

....................................................................................

Meanwhile, warm the mixed grains in a large saucepan, add the lemon juice, tomato paste, and mixed herbs, and season to taste.

....................................................................................

Spoon the grains onto serving plates, arrange the stuffed peppers on top, and serve immediately.

....................................................................................

# SQUASH, CHICKPEA & SWEET POTATO TAGINE

Rich in antioxidants, fiber, and the nerve-boosting B vitamins, this vegetable-packed, fragrant stew is perfect for chilly nights.

**Preparation time:** 25 minutes
**Cooking time:** about 40 minutes
**Serves 4–6**

....................

2 tablespoons **olive oil**
2 **onions**, chopped
2 teaspoons **ground coriander**
2 teaspoons **ground cinnamon**
2 teaspoons **ground cumin**
1 teaspoon **chili powder**
½ inch piece of fresh **ginger root**,
    peeled and grated
3 **garlic cloves**, unpeeled, crushed
1 tablespoon **concentrated tomato paste**
1 large **butternut squash**, peeled,
    seeded, and cut into chunks
2 **sweet potatoes**, peeled and cut
    into chunks
2 **carrots**, cut into chunks
2 **parsnips**, cut into chunks
⅓ cup chopped soft **dried apricots**
3 cups **vegetable stock**
finely grated zest and juice of 1 **lemon**
2 cups rinsed, drained canned **chickpeas**
2 cups coarsely chopped fresh **cilantro**
**sea salt** and **black pepper**
**pomegranate seeds**, to garnish (optional)
**bulgur wheat**, to serve

Heat the oil in a large saucepan over medium heat, add the onions, and cook gently for about 10 minutes, until soft. Stir in the coriander, cinnamon, cumin, chili powder, ginger, and garlic, then the tomato paste.

........................

Cook for another 2–3 minutes, then add the squash, sweet potatoes, carrots, parsnips, and apricots and stir well. Add the stock, lemon zest, and lemon juice, bring to a boil, then reduce the heat and simmer, uncovered, until the vegetables are almost cooked.

...................................

Add the chickpeas and half the fresh cilantro, then season to taste. Cook for another 10–15 minutes, then stir in the remaining cilantro and remove from the heat. Serve immediately with bulgur wheat, sprinkled with pomegranate seeds, if desired.

...........................

# WATERMELON, GINGER & LIME GRANITA

This fresh, light dessert is the ideal way to round off a meal, encouraging restful sleep and easing irritability.

**Preparation time:** 15 minutes, plus cooling and freezing
**Cooking time:** 10 minutes
**Serves 4**

½ cup **lime juice**
6 cups peeled, seeded **watermelon** cubes
finely grated zest of 2 **limes**
⅔ cup **demerara** or **other raw sugar**
2 inch piece of fresh **ginger root**, peeled and finely grated
**mint sprigs**, to decorate

Put the lime juice, watermelon, and half the lime zest in a blender or food processor and blend until smooth. Strain to remove any stray pieces of seed.

Transfer ½ cup of the mixture to a small saucepan, stir in the sugar, the remaining lime zest, and half the ginger, and place over medium heat until the sugar has dissolved. Remove from the heat and let cool.

Stir the cooled syrup into the watermelon puree with the remaining ginger. Pour into a shallow container and freeze for 2 hours, beating with a fork every 20 minutes or so to break up the ice crystals, until it has a thick, slushy consistency. Serve in glass dishes decorated with mint sprigs.

# BRAZIL NUT & BANANA PARFAIT

Rich in protein, the oats and nuts in this sweet, crunchy dessert will help keep blood sugar levels stable.

**Preparation time:** 15 minutes
**Cooking time:** 15 minutes
**Serves 4**

¾ cup **brazil nuts**, chopped
½ cup **maple syrup**
½ cups **rolled oats**
1¾ cups **Greek yogurt with live active cultures**
1 teaspoon **vanilla extract**
1 teaspoon **ground cinnamon**
2 tablespoons **confectioners' sugar**
4 ripe but firm **bananas**, sliced
2 teaspoons **lemon juice**
2 teaspoons **demerara** or **other raw sugar**

Put the brazil nuts and maple syrup in a small saucepan over low heat and cook until the syrup bubbles. Remove from the heat and stir in the oats. Transfer to a nonstick baking sheet and place in a preheated oven, at 325°F, for 10 minutes, or until the oats are toasted and sticky.

Mix the yogurt with the vanilla, cinnamon, and confectioners' sugar and set aside. Reserve 4 slices of banana for decoration, then place the remaining bananas in another bowl with the lemon juice and raw sugar and toss to coat.

Divide half the yogurt mixture among 4 glass bowls or sundae glasses, top with half the bananas, then half the nut mixture. Repeat the layers, finishing with the nut mixture. Decorate with the reserved banana slices and chill until ready to serve.

# ICED BERRIES WITH DARK CHOCOLATE SAUCE

This is possibly the easiest dessert you can make, rich in antioxidants for health and chocolate to raise your spirits.

**Preparation time:** 5 minutes
**Cooking time:** 5 minutes
**Serves 4**
..................

4 oz **semisweet dark chocolate**
½ cup **plain yogurt with live active cultures**
2 tablespoons **confectioners' sugar**,
   plus extra for dusting
4 cups mixed **frozen berries** (raspberries,
   strawberries, blueberries, or blackberries)

Melt the chocolate in a heatproof bowl set over a saucepan of gently simmering water, making sure the water does not touch the bottom of the bowl.
.....................................

Stir in the yogurt and confectioners' sugar and mix until smooth. Sprinkle the frozen berries on 4 serving plates.
.....................................

While the chocolate is still hot, pour the sauce over the frozen berries and dust with a little confectioners' sugar. Serve immediately.
.....................................

# BAKED FIGS WITH MASCARPONE

This is an elegant dessert rich in fiber and calcium. The zesty ginger works both to warm and to aid digestion.

**Preparation time:** 10 minutes
**Cooking time:** 15–20 minutes
**Serves 4**
................

8–12 ripe **figs**, halved
1 tablespoon **butter**, cut into small chunks
2 tablespoons **wild honey**
1 tablespoon packed **dark brown sugar**
1 tsb **ground allspice**
2 teaspoons **ground cinnamon**
finely grated zest and juice of 1 **orange**
½ cup **mascarpone cheese**
½ inch piece of fresh **ginger root**,
   peeled and coarsely chopped
½ teaspoon **vanilla extract**
2 tablespoons **confectioners' sugar**

Arrange the figs in an ovenproof dish, cut side up, and dot with butter. Stir together the honey, sugar, allspice, cinnamon, orange juice, and half the orange zest in a small bowl, and drizzle with the figs. Bake in a preheated oven, at 400°F, for 15–20 minutes, until bubbling.
................

Meanwhile, put the mascarpone, ginger, vanilla, confectioners' sugar, and remaining orange zest into a blender or food processor and blend until smooth and fluffy.
................

Place the figs on serving plates, top each with a spoonful of mascarpone, and drizzle with the fig juices. Serve warm or cold.
................

# DARK CHOCOLATE & RASPBERRY SOUFFLÉ

Don't feel guilty about indulging in this delicious dessert: it will help you relax and lift your mood.

---

**Preparation time:** 10 minutes
**Cooking time:** 20 minutes
**Serves 4**

...............

4 oz **semisweet dark chocolate**
3 **eggs**, separated
⅓ cup **all-purpose flour**, sifted
¼ teaspoon baking powder
⅓ cup **superfine** or **granulated sugar**
1 cup **raspberries**, plus extra
   to serve (optional)
**confectioners' sugar** for dusting

Melt the chocolate in a heatproof bowl set over a saucepan of gently simmering water, making sure the water does not touch the bottom of the bowl. Let cool a little, then beat in the egg yolks and fold in the flour.

............................

Whisk the egg whites and superfine sugar in a clean bowl, using a handheld electric mixer, until they form soft peaks. Beat a spoonful of the egg whites into the chocolate mixture to loosen it, then gently fold in the rest.

...........................................

Divide the raspberries among 4 lightly greased ramekins, pour the chocolate mixture over the berries, then place in a preheated oven, at 375°F, for 12–15 minutes, until the soufflés have risen.

.......................................................

Dust with confectioners' sugar and serve immediately with extra raspberries, if desired.

...................

# TIPSY BLUEBERRY & MASCARPONE DESSERTS

Although alcohol isn't recommended in most mood-lifting menus, a little can lift your spirits and help you relax.

**Preparation time:** 15 minutes, plus soaking
**Serves 4**

1⅓ cups **blueberries**
2 tablespoons **kirsch** or **vodka**
⅔ cup **mascarpone cheese**
⅔ cup **plain yogurt with live active cultures**
2 tablespoons **confectioners' sugar**
finely grated zest and juice of 1 **lime**

Place 1 cup of the blueberries in a bowl, drizzle with the alcohol, and let soak for at least 1 hour. Coarsely mash the soaked blueberries.

Beat together the mascarpone and yogurt until smooth, then stir in the confectioners' sugar, lime zest, and lime juice.

Divide three-quarters of the mashed blueberries among 4 glass serving dishes and top with the mascarpone mixture. Top with the remaining crushed blueberries, sprinkle the whole blueberries on top, and chill until ready to serve.

# CHERRY & NECTARINE MERINGUE

Use nectarines or peaches in this healthy meringue. Instead of the fromage blanc, you can use crème fraîche or Greek yogurt.

**Preparation time:** 20 minutes,
   plus cooling
**Cooking time:** 1 hour
**Serves 4**
...............

3 **egg whites**
¾ cup plus 2 tablespoons **superfine sugar**
1 teaspoon strong black **coffee**
1 teaspoon **vanilla extract**
1 cup **fromage blanc**
1 cup pitted **cherries**
1 **nectarine**, pitted and sliced

Whisk the egg whites in a large bowl with a handheld electric mixer until stiff peaks form. Fold in 1 tablespoon of the sugar, then gradually whisk in the remainder until smooth, glossy, and stiff. Fold in the black coffee and vanilla.
...........................................................

Spoon the meringue onto a baking sheet lined with nonstick parchment paper and spread out to form an 8 inch diameter circle. Make a slight hollow in the center of the meringue and place in a preheated oven, at 250°F, for 1 hour, until the meringue is crisp. Let cool.
...........................................................

Peel the paper off the back of the meringue and place the meringue on a serving plate. Fill the hollow with the fromage blanc and arrange the cherries and nectarine pieces on top. Serve immediately.
...........................................................

# FIG & GRAPE TARTS

These crunchy tarts are simple to make and contain enough fruit to give you an antioxidant and fiber boost.

**Preparation time:** 20 minutes, plus cooling
**Cooking time:** 4 minutes
**Makes 12**

16 sheets **phyllo pastry**
6 tablespoons **butter**, melted, plus extra for greasing
3 tablespoons seedless **raspberry preserves**
2 cups **Greek yogurt with live active cultures**
2 tablespoons **wild honey**
1 teaspoon **vanilla extract**
pinch of **sea salt**
¼ cup **ground almonds**
handful of **blueberries**
handful of seedless **black grapes**, halved
seeds and pulp from 2 **passion fruit**
4 ripe **figs**, quartered
handful of **raspberries**
2 tablespoons **apricot preserves**, warmed

Brush the phyllo pastry sheets, one at a time, with melted butter, then stack them up in a neat pile. Cut the pile into 4–6 squares, depending on their size.

Use the individual pastry squares to line a greased 12-section muffin pan, placing them one on top of the other to line the cups. Offset the pastry squares in each cup to create an uneven, ruched edge.

Place in a preheated oven, at 350°F, for 4 minutes or until the pastry is golden and crisp. Remove from the oven and let cool in the pan for 10 minutes, then transfer the pastry shells to a wire rack to cool completely.

Put the pastry shells onto a serving plate and divide the raspberry preserves among them. Mix the yogurt with the honey, vanilla, salt, and ground almonds in a small bowl and spoon the mixture on top of the preserves.

Arrange the blueberries, grapes, passion fruit, figs, and raspberries in the shells, then brush the tops of the tarts with the warm apricot preserves. Serve immediately.

# TROPICAL FRUIT SALAD WITH GREEN TEA SYRUP

Brimming with antioxidants to ease stress, encourage sleep, and aid digestion, this fruit salad makes a nice breakfast, too!

**Preparation time:** 20 minutes,
   plus infusing and chilling
**Cooking time:** 7 minutes
**Serves 6**
................

2 large **mangoes**, peeled, pitted, and diced
2 large **papaya**, peeled, seeded, and diced
1 small **pineapple**, peeled, cored, and diced
2 **kiwis**, peeled and sliced
2⅔ cups drained canned **lychees**
1⅔ cups **green grapes**

**Syrup**
⅔ cup **sugar**
1¼ cups **water**
grated zest and juice of 1 **lime**
1 inch piece of fresh **ginger root**,
peeled and chopped
1 **green teabag**

To make the syrup, place the sugar, measured water, lime zest, lime juice, and ginger in a saucepan over gentle heat and cook, stirring occasionally, until the sugar has dissolved. Bring to a boil and simmer for 5 minutes.

Remove from the heat and add the teabag, then let steep for 10 minutes. Remove the teabag and pour the syrup into a small bowl. Chill for 10 minutes.

Place all the prepared fruit in a large bowl and strain the cooled syrup over the top. Chill until ready to serve.

# ORANGE, GINGER & SESAME RICE PUDDING

This is a tasty treat, combining warming ginger with brown rice to balance mood and blood sugar.

**Preparation time:** 10 minutes
**Cooking time:** 1¾ hours
**Serves 4**
...............

1⅓ cups **heavy cream**
  or **soy cream**
1¼ cups **water**
½ cup **brown rice**
2 **oranges**
1 inch piece of fresh **ginger root**,
  peeled and grated
3 **egg yolks**
3 tablespoons **demerara** or **other raw sugar**
1 teaspoon **ground cinnamon**
2 teaspoons **vanilla extract**
1 teaspoon **butter**, melted
3 tablespoons toasted **sesame seeds**

Place the cream, measured water, and rice in a large, heavy saucepan and add the juice and finely grated zest of 1 orange. Peel and chop the remaining orange and add to the pan with the ginger.
......................................

Place the saucepan over medium heat, cover, and bring to a boil. Reduce the heat and simmer gently, stirring regularly, for about 1½ hours, until the rice is soft and all of the liquid has been absorbed, adding a little water if it dries out too quickly.
..................................................................

Place the egg yolks in a bowl with the sugar, cinnamon, vanilla, and butter and stir to combine. Add to the pan and cook over low heat, stirring constantly, for 5–10 minutes, until the mixture thickens. Remove from the heat and sprinkle with the sesame seeds. Serve warm or cold.
..................................................................

# CHOCOLATE-DIPPED FRUIT

Chocolate satisfies cravings and, combined with fruit, offers a nutritious snack with maximum feel-good factor.

**Preparation time:** 10 minutes, plus chilling
**Cooking time:** 5–10 minutes
**Serves 4**

...............

3 oz **white chocolate**
3 oz **semisweet dark chocolate**
12 oz **strawberries** with stems
1 cup **cherries** with stems
1 cup **grapes** with stems or toothpicks

Melt the chocolates in 2 separate heat-proof bowls set over saucepans of gently simmering water, being careful to avoid letting the water touch the bottoms of the bowls. Let cool slightly.

.........................................

Dip half the fruit halfway in the dark chocolate, letting the excess to drip back into the bowl. Transfer to a baking sheet lined with nonstick parchment paper to set.

........................................................................

Repeat with the remaining fruit and the white chocolate. Chill in the refrigerator for at least 10–15 minutes, or until ready to eat. Use toothpicks for dipping if the stems are too short.

...............

# POACHED APRICOTS WITH ORANGE FLOWER WATER

The pistachios in this light, fragrant dessert are rich in omega oils and the energy-boosting B vitamins.

**Preparation time:** 10 minutes, plus cooling
**Cooking time:** 5 minutes
**Serves 4**
................

3 cups soft **dried apricots**
1½ cups **apple and elderflower juice**
2 tablespoons **orange flower water**
½ teaspoon **ground cinnamon**
2 tablespoons **honey**
½ cup shelled unsalted
   **pistachios**, crushed
**plain yogurt with live active cultures**
   or **vanilla ice cream**, to serve

Put the apricots, apple and elderflower juice, orange flower water, cinnamon, and honey into a heavy saucepan over medium-high heat and bring to a boil. Reduce the heat and simmer for 2–3 minutes, until the apricots are plump.

....................................

Transfer to a large serving bowl and set aside to cool slightly. Sprinkle with the pistachios and serve warm or cold, with yogurt or ice cream.

....................................

# RESOURCES

**American Foundation for Suicide Prevention**
Tel: (888) 333)AFSP (toll-free)
Tel: (212) 363-3500 (local)
E-mail: inquiry@afsp.org
Web site: www.afsp.org

**American Society for Nutrition**
Tel: (301) 634-7050
Web site: www.nutrition.org

**Anxiety and Depression Association of America**
Tel: (240) 485-1001
Web site: www.adaa.org

**Black Women's Health Imperative**
Tel: (202) 548-4000
E-mail: info@BlackWomensHealth.org
Web site: www.blackwomenshealth.org

**Depression and Bipolar Support Alliance**
Tel: (800) 826-3632 (toll-free)
E-mail: info@dbsalliance.org
Web site: www.dbsalliance.org

**Food and Nutrition Information Center**
Tel: (301) 504-5414
E-mail: FNIC@ars.usda.gov
Web site: fnic.nal.usda.gov

**Freedom From Fear**
Tel: (718) 351-1717 ext. 19
E-mail: help@freedomfromfear.org
Web site: www.freedomfromfear.org

**Mental Health America**
Tel: (800) 969-6642 (toll-free)
Tel: (703) 684-7722 (local)
Web site: www.mentalhealthamerica.net

**National Alliance on Mental Illness**
Tel: (800) 950-6264 (toll-free)
Tel: (703) 524-7600 (local)
Web site: www.nami.org

**National Eating Disorders Association**
Tel: (800) 931-2237 (toll-free)
Tel: (206) 382-3587 (local)
E-mail: info@NationalEatingDisorders.org
Web site: www.nationaleatingdisorders.org

**National Institute of Mental Health**
Tel: (866) 615-6464 (toll-free)
Tel: (301) 443-4513 (local)
E-mail: nimhinfo@nih.gov
Web site: www.nimh.nih.gov/index.shtml

**National Women's Health Network**
Tel: (202) 682-2640
E-mail: healthquestion@nwhn.org
Web site: nwhn.org

**North American Menopause Society**
Tel: (800) 774-5342 (toll-free)
Tel: (440) 442-7550 (local)
E-mail: info@menopause.org
Web site: www.menopause.org

**North American Vegetarian Society**
Tel: (518) 568-7970
Web site: www.navs-online.org

**Postpartum Support International**
Tel: (800) 944-4PPD (toll-free)
tel: (503) 894-9453 (local)
Web site: www.postpartum.net

**Society for Nutrition Education and Behavior**
Tel: (800) 235-6690 (toll-free)
Tel: (317) 328-4627 (local
E-mail: info@sne.org
Web site: www.sne.org

# INDEX

## Acknowledgments

Gill Paul would like to thank the very talented team at Octopus: Denise Bates, who came up with the idea for the series; Jo Wilson, Katy Denny, and Alex Stetter, who edited the books so efficiently and made it all work; and to the design team of Jonathan Christie and Isabel de Cordova for making it all look so gorgeous. Thank you also to Karel Bata for all the support and for eating my cooking.

Karen Sullivan would like to thank Cole, Luke, and Marcus.

## Picture credits

Commissioned photography © Octopus Publishing Group/ Will Heap apart from the following:

**Getty Images**
Anthony Lee 10.

**Octopus Publishing Group**
David Munns 87; Lis Parsons 41, 49, 61, 75, 77, 89, 93, 115; William Shaw 65, 67, 71, 101, 117, 119.

**Thinkstock**
Hemera 16; iStockphoto 5, 7, 8, 9, 12, 18, 21, 22, 27, 34.